WHAT PEOPLE ARI
ABOUT MY WHOLE nani

I really thought I had heard and read pretty much everything related to dealing with the past and the healing of the heart and soul. Then Jo Naughton's manuscript arrived. Sitting on my bed, I found myself weeping. Using the word, her very personal experiences and the testimony of others, Jo gently shepherds the reader through long forgotten pain and into total restoration. Her chapters on guilt, embarrassment and the causes of much of our pain, were just some of my favorite eye-opening reads.

This book is a sacrifice of love from the author. Jo has learned the truths in its pages by walking through many difficult situations that life has thrown at her. I can say with total confidence that this is Jo's best work ever. You will come back to this book again and again and again. My copy is already marked up with pink, yellow and blue markers! Every page is a revelation. Most importantly, the love of God drips off each paragraph like liquid gold. Thank you, Jo, for paying the price.

Prophet Cathy Lechner
Author and International Speaker

Prophet Jo Naughton brings a fresh, practical perspective to the important topic of the supernatural transformation of the spiritual heart in her latest book: *My Whole Heart*. Given that the condition of our heart affects every aspect of our spiritual, emotional, and even physical life, this book is vitally important as it leads the reader to understand how to become spiritually heart-healthy because if our heart is hardened and full of sin, pain, offenses, and unbelief that is exactly what the condition of our life will be as well. None of us can afford to live with a hardened heart as it will deceive us and hinder us from perceiving the voice of God, resulting in a life full of pain, chaos, confusion, and disorder. I highly recommend this book as Prophet Jo provides divine revelation and practical application of the truth of God's Word and the power of the Holy Spirit to take our heart, damaged by our sinful nature, towards a supernatural transformation that we may walk in the fullness of our purpose and destiny in God.

Apostle Guillermo Maldonado
King Jesus International Ministry
Miami, Florida

Many years ago, I experienced a powerful, life changing outpouring of the Holy Spirit. Afterwards, I excitedly talked to the Lord about what had happened and the impact it would have on my ministry. The Lord ignored all my ramblings about gift and anointing and asked me one question, a question which would shape my future: "How is your heart?" This question led me on a pilgrimage towards seeking a right heart. This journey has now lasted 20 years.

This book is a guide for anyone who wants to go on that same journey. It will help you to climb the heights as well as descend into the valleys. It will lead you to green and pleasant pastures. It's one thing to set your heart on pilgrimage but it is another to know how. Jo Naughton has provided 'The Why', 'The Where', and 'The How' in a thoroughly Biblical way. This is quite simply an excellent book that should be read by everyone who is serious about getting their heart right. I thoroughly recommend it to you as you embark on your journey to purity and wholeness.

Apostle Ken Gott
Partners in Harvest
Founder, House of Prayer Europe, Sunderland, England

"As for you, my son Solomon, know the God of your father, and serve Him with a whole heart and a willing mind; for the LORD searches all hearts, and understands every intent of the thoughts If you seek Him, He will let you find Him..." 1 Chronicles 28:9

This extensive collection of spiritually meticulous and thorough insights will enable you to know and serve God with a WHOLE HEART! Jo Naughton offers valuable and practical methods to bring God's loving restoration and wholeness to your heart. This is a book that you will treasure and return to again and again.

Dr. LaDonna Taylor
Psalmist, Violinist and International Speaker

MY WHOLE HEART

JO NAUGHTON

Grosvenor House
Publishing Limited

Book cover design by Freisa Davila

The right of Jo Naughton to be identified as the author of this
work has been asserted in accordance with Section 78
of the Copyright, Designs and Patents Act 1988

This book is published by
Grosvenor House Publishing Ltd
Link House
140 The Broadway, Tolworth, Surrey, KT6 7HT.
www.grosvenorhousepublishing.co.uk

A CIP record for this book
is available from the British Library

ISBN 978-1-78623-268-7

Some names and details have been changed to protect the
identity of the people whose stories are included in this book.
Bible references are from the New King James version unless
otherwise stated. The Message is also used to help reveal
the heart of certain passages.

This book is dedicated to everyone who has joined the journey to wholeness and embraced the Healed for Life movement.

Acknowledgements

My husband, Paul: Thank you for being God's number one tool of transformation in my life.

My children, Benj and Abby: Thank you for being the best and bringing constant joy to my heart.

Pastors Ken and Lois Gott: Thank you for bringing the healing love of the Lord into my life.

Prophet Cathy Lechner: Thank you for believing in me and encouraging me every step of the way.

Apostle Guillermo Maldonado: Thank you for releasing a greater measure of God's glory into my ministry.

Tim Collins: Thank you for investing your wisdom, time and talents in this book.

Healed for Life Warriors and Partners: Thank you to every prayer warrior and monthly giver who is helping bring this precious ministry to the world.

Harvest Church London: Thank you for being the best church family a pastor could ask for.

Mum: Thank you for your love and support down through the decades.

Contents

Introduction

My Whole Heart will take you on a journey to greater peace and freedom. The Holy Spirit will shine His light into your heart as you read and uncover hidden issues that have been holding you back. It is no accident that you have this book in your hand. God is about to begin a brand-new work on the inside that will bring transformation and restoration.

Chapter 1
THE HUMAN HEART

The human heart is vast. Imagine an enormous storage vault filled with filing cabinets. Picture rows of drawers, all packed with files containing infinite numbers of folders. Contained within each binder is a memory, an imagination, or an emotion. Now see the door to that vault. It could be closed. Perhaps there is a 'no entry' sign hanging in the window. It may be ajar. It might be wide open. That is what our hearts are like. Psalm 64:6b in the Amplified says: "... For the inward thought of each one [is unsearchable] and his heart is deep." This might not matter, but it does. The Bible says to "Love the Lord with all your heart". Proverbs 4:23 explains: "Guard your heart above all else, for it determines the course of your life." (New Living Translation). It matters because your vast inner vault decides your destiny.

Out of Nowhere

Have you ever been reminded of an event that you had completely forgotten? Maybe the remarks of family or friends dug up a vivid picture that you hadn't seen for decades. Perhaps a smell or sight took you straight back to a scene which you had long forgotten. Imagine what else is hidden. Our hearts are extensive. There are countless memories, thoughts and feelings hidden inside.

It's not just old memories that get buried. We often detach ourselves from unwanted emotional reactions. Something happens that makes you crumple. Perhaps it is a put-down at work or a stupid mistake. You feel squashed or ashamed. These kinds of feelings are usually desperately unpleasant so instead of facing how you feel, you deny the damage and pretend you are unaffected. And another unexpressed emotion sinks to the bottom of your soul. The result? Your heart is home to a whole host of hidden or forgotten memories which could revisit you at any time.

Alien Thoughts

In the spring of 2005, I was rummaging around in my bedroom. I was sorting myself out for the week ahead when an alien thought popped into my mind. I say alien because it felt as far from my view of my life as you can imagine. It went something like this: "Why did my mum show more love to my sister than to me?" What you need to understand is that, in my opinion, I was a successful, happily married Christian woman who did not have any issues with the past. Yet here I was with a thought dropping into my mind that to me smacked of weakness. I didn't want to think it. In fact, it made me cringe. So, I pushed it away and went about my business. But soon enough, that rogue sentiment popped into my head again.

No matter how strange the thought was, I had to acknowledge that it came from deep inside *me*. Proverbs 20:27 says, "The spirit of man is the lamp of the Lord, searching the inner depths of the heart." It was as though someone had opened up the inner depths of my vault and highlighted an unwanted folder buried under mountains of junk. It brought me back to a time in my childhood that I would rather not have remembered. It stirred up feelings that I would have preferred to forget. I liked to be reminded of my current position. I was a passionate Christian minister and a vice-president of the world's biggest public relations company! I had no desire to go back to times of weakness and failure. I did not want to remember the years of longing for attention as a teenager. However, the Holy Spirit was shining His light into my past for the sake of my future.

Thinking the Unthinkable

Many of us unwittingly categorize our memories. Some recollections are painful, while others are intensely uncomfortable or shameful. Certain old images, although unwanted, may be tolerable. Others could be completely out of bounds. The thoughts that popped into my mind may seem harmless to you. To me, they were horrible.

Despite feeling disgusted, I stopped and spoke to God. "Father, I don't understand where such weird ideas are coming from, but if there is something that I need to face, have Your way." This was the closest I could get to praying the Biblical way: "Search me [thoroughly], O God, and know my heart. Try me and know my thoughts..." (Psalms 139:23 Amplified). I want to encourage you to respond with courage to the memories the Holy Spirit brings to your mind. As with anything, the more we do it, the easier it becomes. When you get used to allowing the Lord to spotlight hidden hurts, it will become natural. He reveals and then He heals.

Before & After

God heard my heart that day and started to unearth pain buried in the recesses of my soul. That was over a decade ago and it marked the very start of my journey to truth and transformation. When I look back over my adult years, there is a vast difference between my life before and after my inner vault was opened to the Lord. Life beforehand was marked by hidden insecurities, relationship upsets and endless efforts to get things right. Life after this journey of restoration began has been wonderful. I'm sure glad that I paused and prayed that day, instead of ignoring the unwelcome reflection. That rogue thought eventually led me on the path to wholeness. I later discovered that someone was praying for me during that season, for God to reveal hidden hurts and to make my heart whole. That is one of the reasons why we allocate an intercessor to everyone who books a place on our Healed for Life courses from the moment they register.

The Door

I don't know whether the door to your inner vault is open or closed. Perhaps the Holy Spirit has been prompting you to surrender. I believe that the fact you are reading this book is no coincidence. Proverbs 3:5 is encouraging: "Trust in the Lord with all your heart and lean not on your own understanding." Trust can be described as the moment when we let go and let God have His way. You can trust God to take care of your heart. He knows how to bring you on a wonderful journey to freedom and rich fulfillment.

Almost Unfathomable

Before I was in full time ministry, I used to offer management coaching to leaders in major organizations. My talent was in helping people who had been newly promoted into senior roles to develop the skills to be a success. I would provide my clients with an analysis of their current strengths and weaknesses and then develop a plan to help them grow.

One topic that we covered was the power of thoughts. We all tend to think on at least two levels. We have our conscious thoughts that are at the forefront of our minds. In addition, we have musings that are beneath the surface. We are not always conscious of those thoughts, yet they have a significant impact upon our performance. I used to call this realm of unconscious thought the twilight zone and I would help my clients develop the right inner thinking.

Psalm 64:6 says, "The inner thought and heart of man are deep." The Hebrew word for inner can also be interpreted as heart. It would therefore be possible to translate this verse as follows: "The heart thought - and heart of man - are deep." This suggests we have different types of thoughts. We have head thoughts, but we also have heart thoughts. Sometimes our heart thoughts are hidden. They are our inner assumptions about ourselves and the world around us. They can be so deep that they don't even have words. They may, at times, be expressed by a sigh or a groan - or they may be completely concealed.

Heart Thoughts

The Bible makes a powerful statement: "As a man thinks in his heart, so is he." (Proverbs 23:7). Our heart thoughts determine how we live our lives. Do you remember old fashioned movie projectors? Perched on a tripod, they would project light through rolling tape onto a screen. That's what our inner thoughts are like. They roll out the movie of our lives. My heart thoughts will determine the person I become. They draw a boundary around my potential to succeed in almost every area of life. If I think I am capable, I will achieve much more than if I doubt my competence.

God has placed great potential on the inside of you to succeed in every area of life. However, if you doubt your ability deep down or you believe you are a disappointment, you will probably struggle to fulfill that potential. Heart thoughts are deep convictions. They are the views you hold, and often unconsciously project, about yourself. These thoughts are molded by life's experiences and are locked away in the filing cabinets of your inner vault. If a teacher told you that you were stupid when you were a child, you may have battled against those words all your life. Those remarks, even if they were spoken decades ago, could still bind you to failure. Those rash words could have become a heart thought that has framed your beliefs and dictated your behavior. Your heart is deep, and it is powerful.

Psalm 49:11 says, "Their inner thought is that their houses will last forever…" Of course, houses never last forever. The psalmist is making the point that we can believe lies which frame our view of life and shape our attitudes. These inner thoughts can mean that, despite every effort to grow in confidence, our self-esteem is in tatters. I believe that you desire to live in greater freedom, so it will be important that you allow God to reveal any heart thoughts that are hampering your life. Psalm 51:6 says that God desires truth in the inward parts. Your inner thoughts come from your inward parts, from the depths of your being, from your heart.

It's All in The Mind

Head thoughts are different. They come as ideas and often influence our attitudes. They are still important because attitude is vital. Also, if we rehearse them for long enough, they too can become heart thoughts. All too often, we try to deal with our head thoughts without addressing our heart thoughts. Heart thoughts are like the driver of a car whereas head thoughts are like a backseat passenger. The passenger can say whatever he wants. If the driver isn't listening, it makes no difference to the direction of travel.

As a teenager, I remember gathering a long list of verses that affirmed my value to God. I would regularly repeat "I am fearfully and wonderfully made", trying desperately to believe the words. However hard I tried, I would still feel inadequate. It was only when God started to heal me deep down that my heart thoughts started to line up with God's word. If all we do is fill our heads with the truth, we will struggle to change. We need to ask God to heal our hearts and renew our inner thoughts so that they help us achieve our potential and please our Heavenly Father.

It's Deep

Let us look again at Psalm 64:6: "The inner thought and heart of man are deep." We have unpacked heart thoughts. The Hebrew word for deep is *amoq*, which means unsearchable, mysterious and exceedingly deep. That's how the Bible describes our thoughts and our soul. There is nothing straightforward about the human heart. Your heart is profound and complex. It is deep and mysterious. Speaking of the heart, the prophet Jeremiah said: "Who can know it [perceive, understand, be acquainted with his own heart and mind]?" (Jeremiah 17:10b Amplified). Did you get that? This verse says that it's very difficult for anyone to really understand what is going on inside. We think we know ourselves, but the truth is that most of us don't. Your heart houses a colossal amount of emotional information that is daily affecting your progress. Most of the time, you will not even realize how hidden heart thoughts are directing your life.

Your Heart Sets Your Course

For me, one of the most important verses in the Bible is Proverbs 4:23. Let's look at it in the NIV: "Above all else, guard your heart, for everything you do flows from it." Everything you do flows from your heart. It is not just your relationships and attitudes that are affected by your heart. Everything that we do is influenced by our inner wellbeing. The New Living Translation makes it crystal clear: "Guard your heart above all else, for it determines the course of your life." It is not my education or my upbringing. It is not my qualifications or my talents. It is my heart that will determine how my life turns out. The condition of my heart sets my course.

There is no doubt that we can do well for a season, despite our inner issues. However, if we want to fulfill our highest potential and enjoy rewarding relationships, our hearts need to be free from all hurts, hindrances, grief, and sorrows. If you want to accomplish your earthly purpose, you will need to do it God's way. We need to become people who will pursue inner purity. We need to take care of our hearts more diligently than we look after anything else. We need to prioritize the wellbeing of our souls because that's how we fight for our future. To God, your heart shouts loudest.

Our hearts are our most important asset and yet most of us have very little insight into our own inner workings. That's why we need to take on board the instruction in Proverbs 4:23 to prioritize our inner lives. That's why we need to open up to God like never before and allow Him to do what only He can do. Our Heavenly Father says, "I, the Lord, search the heart, I test the mind..." (Jeremiah 17:10). Only God can fully understand your reactions, intentions, desires, and imaginations. Only He can minister into your depths and bring about true transformation that sets you up for eternal success.

One of A Kind

There are a multitude of different yet breathtaking landscapes across the earth. From arid deserts to snow-capped mountains, and from packed pine forests to barren, heather-filled moors. Every scene is unique. In the same way, each one of our hearts is completely different. Your heart is exceptional and one of a kind. Psalm 33:15 says, "He fashions their hearts individually." He crafted and formed your inner depths. Your soul is not a clone. One of the reasons why relationships can be so tricky is that every human heart is unique. Your hopes and dreams, your desires and aversions, your loves and likes are individual. Your sister or spouse is not the same. Differences can create misunderstandings and friction. The only one who completely understands and identifies with your every inner sigh is your loving Creator.

Out of His desire for your success, God wants you and I to learn to hear the cries and concerns of our hearts. Proverbs 20:5 says that, "The purposes of a person's heart are deep waters, but a man of understanding draws them out." (NIV) Our thoughts are deep; our intentions are complex, and our reactions are often uncomfortable. Memories can evoke anger, pain, or shame. So why would an insightful man or woman even want to draw out things that may be best left alone? As we have already said, our hearts determine the course of our lives. If we leave hidden hurts, they will probably affect the way we live our lives. If we ignore old issues, they may rear their heads when they are most unwanted. We need to allow God to work on our hearts so that our lives can bring more glory to His name.

The Power of The Truth

Linda grew up in a Christian home, but there was constant conflict in her family. Her dad and sister were always arguing - often yelling - and so she became the peacemaker. Without realizing it, she developed a habit of constantly trying to keep everyone happy. Whether it was at school or at church, that was her role in friendship groups. Not only that, but she was always trying to please teachers, leaders and her parents. Unhealed hidden hurts forged deep-rooted heart thoughts which motivated her behavior. It was exhausting, but she had absolutely no idea why she felt constantly compelled to pacify and please. She thought it was just her personality.

Linda attended our two-day conference called Healed for Life. While she was with us, God showed Linda just how much she had been hurt by all the friction at home. When we feel it, God will heal it. She cried like never before and felt unbelievably relieved afterwards. Then on day two, she was set free from worrying about what other people thought. She left Healed for Life feeling free. She was free to express herself and free to be herself. Peace reigned. Since then, Linda has continued on her healing journey.

We Reflect our Maker

The Bible says that our thoughts are deep. However, Psalm 92:5 says of God: "Your thoughts are *very* deep." There is a depth to the heart of God and an expanse to His thoughts that far outweigh human understanding. Deep thoughts are therefore a good thing, but they are best when they can be expressed. God's meditations are not only vast in scale. His ability to express Himself is breathtaking. Our Lord is constantly communicating by His Spirit, through prophets and preachers, and in the wonder and beauty of creation.

"How precious are Your thoughts to me Oh God! How great is the sum of them! If I should count them, they would be more in number than the sand..." (Psalm 139:17-18). God's heart is enormous, and His emotional capacity is colossal. His thoughts towards you are full of feeling. Very often, our thoughts trigger our feelings. Occasionally, emotions pop up without any prompting, but normally our musings produce our emotional reactions. That is because we are made in God's image. His thoughts trigger a whole host of amazing emotions.

Your Heart Matters

Heart disease can be terminal and heart failure often signals the end of life. In the same way, inner issues can produce major problems and a shutdown can lead to spiritual death. I hope by now that you understand it is vital that you prioritize your heart. We have already touched on the first, but here are five foundational reasons why your heart needs to be made whole.

1. Your Destiny

God does not see as man sees. Man looks at the outward appearance, whilst God looks at the heart. When the Lord is looking for a man or woman that He can promote, He considers the state of our hearts. We have already talked about Proverbs 4:23. It is so important that I want to recap by looking at it in the Amplified: "Keep and guard your heart with all vigilance and above all that you guard, for out of it flow the springs of life." This verse is telling us to prioritize our hearts above all else for the sake of our future. It explains that our very lives flow from the issues of our hearts. The state of our hearts determines how our lives will turn out. God has wonderful, deeply fulfilling plans for your life. He wants to promote you and enable you to achieve great things. However, the extent to which we achieve our true God-given potential will depend upon the condition of our hearts. Hurts, buried pain and disappointments can all too easily hinder our progress.

2. Your Prosperity

From the beginning of time, we see God's heart is to prosper His people. The Hebrew word for prosper is ṣâlaḥ. It means to push forward, break out mightily and to be profitable. In its essence, it means to thrive in every area of life. As soon as God entered a covenant with people, He started to prosper them. Abraham was blessed beyond measure with land and livestock and ended up with a massive number of employees helping him to administer his business. Psalm 35:27 tells us that the Lord takes pleasure in prospering His people. He wants you to flourish in your spiritual life, family life, health, ministry and work or business. So, what has this got to do with the heart? 3 John 1:2 says, "Beloved, I pray that you may prosper in all things and be in health, just as your soul prospers." The Holy Spirit is praying through the apostle John that you would prosper to the extent that your soul prospers. Remember that the Biblical definitions for heart and soul are very similar. Here we have another verse, this time in the New Testament, reinforcing the fact that the condition of our soul will impact our life – especially our prosperity and health. This makes it clear that the more we are sound and sorted on the inside, the more we will thrive in every area of life.

3. Faith to Grow

It is impossible to please God without faith. We lay hold of all the promises in Scripture by faith. The Lord has designated faith as the currency of His kingdom. You need money to buy the things you need on earth. You wouldn't go into a store and try to pay with potatoes. Vegetables are nutritious and have value, but you cannot use them to make purchases. You need dollars. In the same way, the Lord has established His kingdom with a currency called faith. If we are going to grow in God and possess His many promises, we can only do so with faith. If we are going to fulfill our God-given potential, we need faith. This makes faith vital.

Romans 10:9 tells us where faith abides: "... if you... believe in your heart..." Faith is of the heart. Our thoughts affect our beliefs, but faith grows deep inside. If my heart is heavy or hurting, it will be hard to grow my faith. If I'm sad or disappointed, it will be difficult to develop my belief. Sometimes, we think we are full of faith but in truth we are grasping at straws and trying to convince ourselves that everything will be well. That is often because underneath all our confessions and prayers, there are a whole host of heart issues that need to be resolved.

4. True Hope

The Bible says that faith is the substance of the things for which we hope (Hebrews 11:1). The way to grow faith is to build your hope because faith comes alive where there is hope. In the same way that ice is made from freezing water, you develop faith by nurturing hope. The Biblical explanation of hope is different to the world's definition. It is not wishful thinking. True hope is the confident expectation that we will receive the things that the Bible promises. Faith is when we "know that we know" that we have got what we have been asking for in prayer. It announces its presence in that moment when victory arises on the inside of you - even before anything changes on the outside. Just as we need our hearts to be right to have faith, we need to be in a good place deep within to have hope.

The Bible says in James 1:15 that "...desire gives birth". What does that mean? Desire is compelling. It motivates us to fulfill our mandate. It propels us to go after our dreams. It creates the determination we need to keep going. Desire is one of the fruits of hope and it lives and grows in our hearts. If you are discouraged, it can drown your desire. If you are feeling rejected or betrayed, it can choke your motivation to pursue your purpose. Some people are weighed down with regret, causing them to look backwards rather than forwards. We need our hearts to be free from issues like this for hope's sake.

5. Unconditional Love

God is love and we are called to walk in love towards those around us. When we show love, it proves we belong to Jesus: "By this all will know that you are My disciples, if you have love for one another." John 13:35. Faith, hope and love will remain when every spiritual gift is no longer necessary. But 1 Corinthians 13:13 tells us that love is the greatest of these three enduring kingdom values.

Love is not self-seeking. It does not prioritize its own needs. Instead, it seeks the well-being of others. Love believes the best. Think about this for a moment. Now consider how you feel when someone really hurts you. Perhaps a brother betrayed you and left you with overwhelming business debts. Maybe a leader let you down or crushed your confidence. A friend might have broken their promises. We know that we need to forgive. However, in truth that is not enough. You see, when I forgive someone, I can let go of what they did but I will probably be wary of any contact. My buried wounds will make it almost impossible for me to be warm and caring. To walk in love, I need my heart to be healed. The kind of love we are called to demonstrate to the people around us is unconditional. It is patient, it is kind and it believes the best. For you to show that kind of love towards those who have hurt you, your heart needs to be made whole.

What Next?

I encourage you to make a decision. Choose to open your heart to a brand-new work of the Holy Spirit. Make a commitment to prioritize the condition of your heart. We have established that our souls are unique, deep and that we don't always know them like we thought we did. Not only that, the state of our souls determines the nature of our lives. I would love to lead you in prayer...

Heavenly Father,

I open up my heart again to You today. I ask You to shine Your light into the depths of my heart over the coming days and weeks as I read this book. I open up every room of my heart to You. I give You permission to do what You need to do in me so that I might be made whole on the inside. I choose today to prioritize my heart. I surrender to Your Spirit and I surrender to Your love. Have Your way in my heart, I pray.

In Jesus' name,

Amen.

Chapter 2
THE HEART KNOWER

God is acquainted with every memory stored in every folder of every filing cabinet in the vault of your heart. He sees every sigh of your soul. The Lord understands all your thoughts - both those that are conscious and those that are hidden. He fully understands your feelings, your passions and your aversions. He knows what motivates you and what causes you to shut down. The Lord can tell how you are going to respond to any and every situation, even when you do not know yourself. He gets you.

At the start of the book of Acts, the disciples were deciding who should replace Judas after he tragically took his own life. They wanted to appoint a twelfth apostle and had two potential candidates. They fasted and then prayed: "You, Lord, Who know all hearts (their thoughts, passions, desires, appetites, purposes, and endeavors), indicate to us which one of these two You have chosen." (Acts 1:24 Amplified). The phrase "Who know all hearts" is not four words in the original Greek. It is one word, kardiognōstēs, which means heart-knower. The apostles called God the Heart-knower. He knew their hearts and He knows yours.

Psalms 139:13 says: "You formed my inward parts..." Inward parts is a Hebrew word kilya, which is often translated as heart or mind. Yes, God put every organ, artery and vein in place. However, what is just as important is that God formed your soul. He designed and created your innermost being. He made your unique, complex, inward parts. No wonder He understands your thoughts and reactions. Where Psalm 139:2 says, "You understand my thought afar off," the Lord knows every one of your reflections and understands why they matter to you. God recognizes what you are thinking right now. He knows you completely and He loves you perfectly.

Pushing Buttons

When Jesus met the woman at the well in John 4, they had a fairly short conversation. After chatting about worship and water, Jesus told her to call her husband. She replied saying that she didn't have one. Jesus then touched a nerve. He responded, "You have spoken truly in saying, 'I have no husband.' For you have had five husbands, and the man you are now living with is not your husband." (John 4:17-18).

The woman went back to her city and told everybody that she had met a man who told her *everything* she ever did. Jesus did not tell her everything. However, He spoke about the one thing that caused her constant concern. He addressed her elephant in the room. This poor lady must have felt like a total failure. Divorce was rare at this time in history. She was obviously desperate to be loved and yet repeatedly failed in romantic relationships. Jesus is God and God is love. So, when Jesus spoke, love spoke. The Samaritan did not hear judgment. She met love. In that brief encounter, the Lord showed this lady that He knew her completely - warts and all - and yet loved her unconditionally.

Our Savior is fully aware of every one of your inner struggles. The Bible says: "God... is acquainted with and understands the heart..." Acts 15:8. When you are acquainted with someone, you can predict their responses and reactions to different situations. He knows exactly how you are feeling and what you are facing.

Although at times, like that lady, we talk to God about water and worship, He knows what is going on deep down. He knows the things that are causing you concern. He understands what makes you recoil or churn. Jesus bypassed the Samaritan's distractions and went straight to the core of her problems. In the same way, He wants to deal with your real issues. He does not reveal secrets to embarrass you but to help you. The Samaritan woman did not feel exposed. She felt known and she was set free. The Lord sees the burdens that are weighing you down and is able to lift them from your shoulders. He feels your buried pain and is waiting to heal. He recognizes the pressure building up inside you and is ready to relieve it.

Revealing Secrets

Even when Jesus was just a baby, we are told that part of His mission as an adult would be to bring to light our hidden thoughts and feelings. A devout Jew called Simeon prophesied over Mary the mother of Jesus, saying: "A sword will pierce through your own soul also, that the thoughts of many hearts may be revealed." (Luke 2:35). Mary suffered the excruciating pain of seeing her son die so that our hearts could be unlocked. Jesus came (in part) to expose the issues buried in our hearts so that He could heal them. He is deeply committed to our inner wholeness. The Lord wants to help us become honest about what is going on inside because truth is the way to freedom: "You shall know the truth and the truth shall set you free." (John 8:32). On at least seven occasions in the Gospels, Scripture tells us that Jesus knew the thoughts of the hearts of the people. Because Jesus understood what was really going on inside, He could address the genuine issues of people's lives. He knew them, and He knows you right now.

In the Old Testament, God sent prophets to shed light on the affairs of His people's hearts. Daniel made this statement: "This secret has not been revealed to me because I have more wisdom than anyone living, but that… you may know the thoughts of your heart." God sent His servant Daniel to speak to one of his people so that the concerns of his heart could be revealed and then resolved. Very often, you and I don't know what is going on deep inside unless the Spirit of God reveals it to us. God does not look at all the paraphernalia of your life, He looks at your heart. People judge based on what they see but God looks beyond your circumstances. "He reveals the deep and secret things." (Daniel 2:22). He highlights hidden hurts and He uncovers buried trauma. He reveals and then He heals so that we can be free.

Opening Up to The Truth

If you will deliberately open your heart to the Lord, He will show you the issues that you did not even realize were hindering your progress. Proverbs 20:27 says, "The spirit of a man is the lamp of the Lord, searching all the inner depths of his heart." You never have to search for something unless it is hard to find. This verse once again underlines the complexity of your heart. The Holy Spirit desires to shine His light into the recesses of your soul. He wants to open up your inner vault and disarm old hidden memories lurking in the shadows. He reveals so that He can heal. He uncovers so that He can deliver.

Jesus said "I am the way, the truth and the life" in John 14:6 and one of the names of the Holy Spirit is the Spirit of Truth. God is truth and He longs for us to embrace truth in the depths of our hearts: "Behold You desire truth in the inward parts" (Psalm 51:6). The Hebrew word for inner parts also means inner recesses or hidden places. We serve a God who holds truth and transparency very close to His heart. He doesn't want us to avoid or glaze over difficulties. The Lord wants us to be honest with ourselves and with Him.

19

The Arch Liar

The devil is the author of lies. Speaking of satan, Jesus said, "… there is no truth in him. When he speaks a falsehood, he speaks what is natural to him, for he is a liar [himself] and the father of lies and of all that is false." (John 8:44b Amplified). The devil works overtime to drag us into his warped world of deceit. He wants us to live with lies in our lives. The devil wants you to feel safe with secrecy and be afraid of the truth. If you feel more comfortable keeping your life as private as possible, it might be worth asking why. If you allow the Lord to trace the reasons back to their roots, you may find that these habits developed in you after you were wounded or betrayed. Maybe you saw it happen to someone you loved, and you vowed that it would never happen to you. God wants to heal every hurt in our hearts so that we can live life the kingdom way. Deception comes in many forms. Of course, there are outright lies. However, there are many other examples of how deceit can creep into our lives. God always wants to lead us to the truth.

Rebekah's Request

If you have read my other books, or have been to Healed for Life, you may have heard me make reference to 'Rebekah's Request'. Rebekah was married to Abraham's son Isaac and her story is told in the book of Genesis. She asked God a critical question. In my view, it is one of the most insightful and pivotal prayers in Scripture. After years of believing God for a baby, Isaac and Rebekah discovered they were going to be parents. No doubt they were overjoyed. However, as the pregnancy progressed, something felt wrong. We don't know whether she was in pain or if she was just churning. Whatever was going on inside, it didn't feel right, so Rebekah inquired of the Lord: "If all is well, why am I like this?" (Genesis 25:22b). The Lord revealed the reason for her rumblings: she was carrying twins.

'So the women sang as they danced, and said: "Saul has slain his thousands, and David his ten thousands." Then Saul was very angry, and the saying displeased him; and he said, "They have ascribed to David ten thousands, and to me they have ascribed only thousands. Now what more can he have but the kingdom?" So, Saul eyed David from that day forward.' (1 Samuel 18:8). Saul was suspicious of David's every move from that moment onwards. David, in contrast, was still dedicated to him and remained loyal. Saul's heart lied to him and he swallowed it hook, line and sinker.

King Saul spent the next ten years listening to these inner lies and daily tried to kill David. Lies may feel easier in the moment. It probably would have been hurtful and humiliating for Saul to admit to himself (and to God) that he felt threatened and inadequate. However, the truth sets us free. If Saul had allowed the Lord to shine His light into his heart and reveal what was really going on inside, Bible history may have told us a different story about him.

Subtle Lies

Our hearts often tell us that other people are our problem when really our issues are within. We blame others without realizing that our own insecurities are causing our concerns. I love to raise up leaders. A few years ago, a woman that I had trained started to shine. She had become a phenomenal mentor, a great leader and a brilliant preacher. It was a joy to see her grow strong. A season came which took me away from home for long periods of time. This lady was able to step into the breach and fill my shoes. Soon, I started to feel suspicious of her motives. I became wary and I worried that she was vying for my role. Nothing about her behavior had changed, yet I started to read rebellion into her words and actions.

One day, as I prayed, the Lord reminded me of the story of Saul and David. The Spirit showed me that insecurity had crept into my heart and I had listened to the lies of the enemy. I felt threatened because I suspected that this lady was a better mentor than me. I wept as I repented. It should be my goal for those I train to become greater than me. That is the heart of a parent. The scales fell from my eyes and I saw the loyalty of this lady once more. I then brought my insecurity to the Lord in prayer. The Heart-Knower revealed the truth and a destiny relationship was saved. Today this wonderful woman continues to shine. She has grown from strength to strength and now trains many other mentors.

Unanswered Questions

God hears every prayer of your heart. If you are waiting for some answers, remember that delay is not denial. Perhaps He is saving His response for the right moment. My husband and I lost our first daughter just before her second birthday. Her name was Naomi. At the time, she was our only child. The terrible, sudden tragedy broke our hearts into tiny pieces. We were overwhelmed with agony. In the weeks and months after she passed away, God started to heal our shattered lives. I encountered the Lord's supernatural love in the most extraordinary ways. He reached into the depths of my innermost being and literally pulled pain out. Through a series of dramatic and gentle encounters in His presence, my Heavenly Father began to restore my soul. In less than a year, the impossible had happened: virtually all sadness had been dispelled and our broken hearts were made whole.

Although my heart was healed, as the years went by I silently wondered why heaven had been quiet about the death of our daughter. Prophets would come and go from our church but none of them would hear God about our terrible tragedy. It was not a major issue for me. I merely wondered why the Lord had been silent about something so catastrophic. Eleven years after Naomi went to be with the Lord, an American prophet named Cathy Lechner visited our church. She knew nothing of our lives. At the end of the final service of the conference, she asked to pray for people with certain medical challenges. Our daughter Abby fit the description, so I asked someone to pick her up from children's church and bring her to the altar. Prophet Cathy went down the line praying for people, then paused when she reached Abby. She started to prophesy.

The Sighs of Our Souls

At first, Prophet Cathy gave a string of accurate words of knowledge about her education and schooling and then she stopped. "Oh Lord, I hope I'm hearing you," she sighed. She continued, slowly, but very deliberately: "Your sister in heaven is looking down at you. The destiny she was due to fulfill, you will fulfill. Your own and hers. The anointing she was due to carry, you will carry. Your own and hers. It was never the will of the Lord for her to go so soon, but He will turn it around for good." There was not a dry eye in the house (that is except for Abby, who wondered what all the fuss was about!). I was weeping, my husband was weeping, the whole church was weeping. Heaven spoke, and we heard. God did not stop there. One year later, the Holy Spirit sent another prophet, Shawn Bolz, to our church. He gave a very similar word about our daughter in heaven. We were left in no doubt about the heart of God towards us.

Scripture says, "And thus the secrets of his heart are revealed; and so, falling down on his face, he will worship God and report that God is truly among you." (1 Corinthians 14:25). That day, heaven answered the unspoken questions hidden in my heart. I felt understood to a new depth. I realized that the Lord was sensitive to every sigh of my soul. As you open up to His work in your heart, He will show you just how well He knows you. He is aware of every struggle you face and has a plan for your well-being. "The Lord is near... to all who call upon Him in truth." (Psalm 145:18). As you seek Him with your heart held open to the truth, He will draw near like never before.

The Way to Freedom

When we face the truth, we can address the real issues of our hearts, get healed and set free. When we blame others for our issues, deny our mistakes, neglect our hurts and generally bury pain or shame, we remain bound. Facing the truth is the way to freedom and a vital part of becoming whole.

Someone recently told me that they had been avoiding going to Healed for Life. "I don't like pain," a young woman explained. "I just don't want to experience any agony." The irony is that the only pain we feel when we get healed is the pain already buried deep within. The devil lies to us, suggesting that avoiding the truth shields us from our old wounds. Refusing to face the pain of the past only keeps us trapped. I told that lady that she was being hampered by her hurts daily and that it was time to be free. She booked a space at Healed for Life, got healed, was refreshed and experienced a lightness she had never known before. Don't listen to the devil. Pain is always better out than in.

God Knows...

God knows your heart. He sees your hidden hurts and understands your reactions. He appreciates the impact that your backstory has had on your life. Even when your closest friends are fooled by your smiles, He sees the sadness beneath the surface. He knows you and He understands you. I encourage you to invite the Spirit of Truth to search your soul. Give Him access to every area of your heart. Allow the Heart-Knower to uncover the issues on the inside so that you can be made free and whole. Let's pray.

Heavenly Father,

I thank You that You know me completely. You know my thoughts before I think them, and You understand me. You recognize my struggles and You discern all my motives. You know why I do what I do and say what I say. You recognize the root reasons for all my reactions. So, I ask You to search my heart and reveal the hindrances deep within. I open up to You because I know You are good and You want me to be free to fulfill my purpose. As I read this book, shine Your light deep within and bring truth, healing and freedom. Have Your way, I pray.

In Jesus' name,

Amen.

Chapter 3

HOW WHOLE IS YOUR SOUL?

Frank is a wonderful pastor and businessman from Florida. He is a loving husband and a dedicated father. However, he had one issue that repeatedly hurt him and his family. The smallest of slips would cause Frank to snap. This mild-mannered man would unexpectedly erupt in anger at, for example, a broken plate or a spilt drink. Proverbs 27:4 in the Amplified says, "Wrath is cruel, and anger is an overwhelming flood..." Frank understood the hurt that his outbursts were causing and was desperate to be free. He went to deliverance conferences and inner healing retreats but remained unchanged.

The Disconnect

As a baby, Frank was highly active. As soon as he could walk, he would run in every direction! Frank's mother was suffering from the stress of living in a foreign land where she was unable to speak the language. When Frank was just one year of age, his fraught mom began smacking her little boy. Constant spankings caused something to break inside his soul. The active toddler shut down and became withdrawn. Troubled by the change in his personality, Frank's parents took him to the hospital assuming he was sick. After three weeks, he was discharged from the pediatric unit because the medical staff could not find anything wrong with him. From that time on, Frank was subdued. At twelve years of age, Frank lost his mom to cancer. Although he felt empty, he never cried.

Frank suspected that his outbursts of anger were probably rooted in his upbringing. However, he had very few childhood memories and could not connect with past hurts. In his early sixties and after forty years as a Christian, Frank came to Healed for Life. During a session ministering to people with broken emotions, God did a profound work. The Holy Spirit took Frank back to his childhood. He saw the tiny toddler who was beaten. He fell to his knees, wept and hugged the little boy that he was seeing in the spirit. He felt so much love for this tiny child. The healing power of God moved, and Frank's heart was flooded with love and joy. God healed this precious man's broken emotions.

On returning home, Frank described his new-found freedom: "I feel connected with my emotions. I now react normally to everyday situations. Things that would once have made me angry no longer affect me. I can deal with friction without pressure building up. My wife and children have all seen the difference and of course they are delighted! I have found real peace within."

Your Soul

Think of your soul as your headquarters, teeming with activity and directing most of your behavior. Psuche is the Greek word for soul and it refers to your mind, your will and your emotions. Your mind is the place where you process thoughts, respond to motives and unleash your imagination. It is the home of your reason, rationale and memory. It is your intellect. Your will enables you to make choices and decisions. It controls your voluntary actions. Your emotions, of course, are your feelings - ranging from sadness to joy and from loneliness to anger. They also include your desires, affections and aversions.

The Soul Of The Lord

We are made in the image of God. According to the Bible, He is a Spirit and He has a soul. His mind, will and emotions all work exceptionally well. It is important that we grasp how God's soul functions so that we can truly understand how our souls were intended to work. Let us consider the soul of our Creator and Heavenly Father for a moment...

His Mind

The Lord thinks, reasons and imagines. Our first introduction to God is incredible: "In the beginning, God created the heavens and the earth." (Genesis 1:1). The whole earth consists of ice-capped mountains, meandering rivers, arid deserts, dense forests, vast oceans and lush jungles. It is an expression of His breathtaking imagination. You and I were born out of His colorful creativity. Jeremiah 29:11 tells us that our Heavenly Father thinks about us, His children, and develops plans to prosper and bless each one of us.

His Will

God makes excellent, timely and courageous choices. After forming the earth and filling the sea, the land and the air with a vast array of creatures, God made a bold decision: "Let us make man in Our image, according to Our likeness..." (Genesis 1:26). He chose to make us in His image and gave us a soul - just like our Creator. Despite knowing our weaknesses, the Lord chooses to believe in you and me. He will never give up on you because He picked you before He laid the foundations of the earth (Ephesians 1:4).

His Emotions

Our Heavenly Father feels deeply. He freely expresses a whole host of different emotions. There are countless passages in the

Old and New Testaments where God shows love, joy, grief, regret, sadness, anger, compassion and so on. The Lord poured His heart and soul into humanity, but we let Him down. The first time we see God expressing grief is in Genesis 6:6: "And the Lord was sorry that He had made man on the earth, and He was grieved in his heart." Our Heavenly Father felt the pain of disappointment and betrayal. Throughout the Bible, He expresses the whole spectrum of emotion.

We were designed in the image of our Maker. God's will is that you and I should enjoy a fully functioning soul. Just as Jesus died to provide healing and health for your body, so He paid the price for you to have an effective, sound soul. We can have a competent mind, a strong submitted will and real emotional freedom.

Does It Work?

There is a speed monitor in my village. Its sole purpose is to encourage traffic to stick to the speed limit. When you drive past one of these monitors within the limit, it should show a big smiley green face and then display your speed. When you drive too quickly, it should flash an angry red face and tell you how fast you are driving. Unfortunately, that monitor can't read speed! If I drive past whilst over the limit (which of course I never do!), it smiles at me and flashes a slower speed than the one I was traveling at. It looks like it is working because it flashes, smiles and scowls. However, it is well and truly broken.

Our souls can be the same. You may discover as you read that your soul does not work the way it should. You may have a highly functioning mind or will, but in certain areas you have impaired emotions. Perhaps you have uncontrollable outbursts of anger or you may struggle to express sadness. It could be that you don't feel much at all. On the other hand, you may have a squashed will or a damaged mind. Even if these are not your experiences, you might find that you are reading about someone you love. Let's look at how our souls can be damaged.

Your Emotional Profile

You may be aware that you have hurts and pains buried inside. However, you rarely feel the pain. You know that you have issues that need to be addressed but you feel detached from what happened. Sometimes, when you look back at your life it is almost as if it happened to someone else. Alternatively, you might think you are fine. You know what you went through but consider yourself to have escaped relatively unscathed. You don't believe that you were especially affected by your upbringing. However, you do know that there should be a greater sense of fulfillment in your life. By contrast, certain emotions may be all over the place: too much, too often. There are many different types of broken emotion. You may feel nothing, very little, too much, or the wrong stuff. Psalm 143:3 describes the damage that the enemy tries to do to our souls: "For the enemy has persecuted my soul; he has crushed my life to the ground..." Satan is always seeking to spoil our souls so that he can limit our lives. Below I describe some of the ways our emotions can be damaged. You might fit the profile of one category or you could see something of yourself in several. If any of this resonates, please simply acknowledge that you need to be healed. It is the first step on your journey to wholeness.

1. Numb

Maybe you are numb. You have gone through so much trauma and pain that your memories blur. Speaking of God's people in Psalm 107:5, the Bible says, "...their soul fainted in them..." Perhaps something on the inside of you has lost consciousness. When you look back at your past, it is as though you are watching some other child suffer. It seems as though it all happened to someone else. You probably still get sad, frustrated or angry, but you cannot express your emotions in a healthy manner. The Psalmist recognized that the temptation to shut down on the inside can sometimes be so great that God alone has to keep us: "Unless the Lord had been my help, my soul would have settled in silence" (Psalm 94:17). The writer clearly understood that shutting down on the inside is dangerous. He recognized that he needed the Lord's help to acknowledge and express his true inner feelings. You see, satan likes us to express negative emotions as long as we don't deal with them properly. But the enemy hates it when we deal with our pain. The devil tries to make you bury your sadness deep within. If this describes you, God wants to heal your soul.

Raquel grew up in a horribly hostile home. There were no kind conversations - only yelling, rage and violence. From a very young age, Raquel was physically and sexually abused by extended family members. "I never heard the words 'I love you'", Raquel explained. "All I ever knew was hatred and hurt. Every single day, my mom tore me apart with verbal attacks and beatings." By the age of five, Raquel had learned to detach herself from her emotions to avoid the agony. She hardly ever spoke.

Tell Tale Signs of Trauma

As an adult, Raquel always felt rejected. She became a Christian when she was 19 but continued to carry pain deep within. Whether they came from family or friends, even small remarks caused her to crumple. She would feel under attack during disagreements and at a loss for words in challenging discussions. Although she could cry a little, she felt like everything was tightly shut within. When the presence of God descended, she struggled to be completely vulnerable. "I didn't even have the vocabulary to express what I felt in my depths," Raquel continued. "I couldn't remember many of the painful experiences of my past. It was as though those memories were locked away, out of reach, and yet they still wore me down daily."

Although the Holy Spirit started a wonderful work during her first healing conference, it was at Raquel's second Healed for Life that God ministered to her like never before. As we prayed for people with broken emotions, the Holy Spirit took Raquel back to when she was five. "When I saw myself as a little girl in prayer, all I could hear were the awful words of worthlessness spoken over me. I thought I was ugly. I could hear myself telling that little girl, 'I hate you!' Then the healing began! I was overwhelmed by the presence of God."

For the first time in her life, Raquel broke down as the dam of agony deep within burst its banks. From the depths of her heart, she cried in God's presence and poured out pain that had been buried for decades. Looking back on the experience, Raquel said, "As the hurts came rushing out, God's love became so real and vivid. I loved that instance. That was my favorite moment." Since that time, Raquel has felt an inner security like never before. When hurtful things happen, there is a peace deep down that won't let her dwell on the rejection. Summing it all up, Raquel concluded: "I am so grateful for what God did at Healed for Life. It is so supernatural. I feel free to be me."

2. Detached

Maybe you have emotional reactions, but on the whole you're quite detached. You may be a decent person, but when others suffer it doesn't touch you the way it affects some. You don't automatically empathize with other folk and the problems they face. When it comes to your own emotions, it is all very contained. You don't talk much about how you feel. Joshua 6:1 describes a fortified city: "Now Jericho was securely shut up because of the children of Israel; none went out, and none came in." The place had massive walls around it to protect itself from invasion. That may be a picture of your emotions: locked away. You probably shut down during your childhood to protect yourself from more pain. Nowadays, you may shed a tear watching a movie, but you don't weep when you or others are wounded emotionally. In contrast, the Apostle Paul "wept freely" as he said goodbye for the last time to his Ephesian brothers (Acts 20:37). Jesus cried when He saw the pain of others. Being connected with our emotions enables us to give and receive love. If you are detached, the Lord wants to bring restoration.

3. Not Very Emotional

Have you ever heard someone say, "I'm not a very emotional person"? Perhaps that is you. You think of yourself as someone whose feelings are somewhat confined. Is it just the way that you were made or is something else going on? Of course, there are differences in how we express ourselves. Some people are bubbly and others are calm. However, every one of us was originally created with the freedom to express our feelings. When you say that you are not very emotional, you probably mean that you don't often feel or express pain. You do have feelings, but you often muffle your emotions. You rarely cry when you have been hurt. You probably have a sense of sadness beneath the surface and may (as a result) battle with dryness or discouragement.

When someone says that they are hard of hearing or they have poor eyesight, we know that they have a problem that affects their lives. In truth, saying "I'm not very emotional" is admitting that your soul isn't working properly. A God-given inner function needs fixing. Just as a blocked artery can cause heart problems, stifled emotions can stagnate the soul and impair our quality of life.

The enemy may have fed you the lie that expressing sadness is a sign of weakness. Satan wants you to believe that constraining emotion is a strength. But that is what the devil does. It is not what God does. Joseph was one of Israel's greatest leaders. He was both strong and sensitive. In just seven chapters of Genesis, he cried seven times. He wept alone, in the arms of his father and his brothers. Joseph was astute, tough and tender. In the same way, God wants you to have fully functioning emotions.

4. Gushing

You may be at the other end of the spectrum. You are overly emotional. Have you ever shaken a bottle of soda and then slowly unscrewed the lid? The fizzy liquid gushes out, causing quite a commotion. When you have lots of unhealed hurts on the inside, the slightest thing can cause you to crack. All too often, you get upset about the things that don't really matter because you haven't faced the deep-rooted hurts. You overreact to the normal behavior of the people around you, often driving those who love you away. Proverbs 25:28 says, "Whoever has no rule over his own spirit is like a city broken down..." When we have no control over our feelings, our emotions are generally broken.

That was me. My emotions were all over the place. I saw everything through the lens of my damaged soul and cried far too often over silly matters. I spilled emotions over my closest family and friends. My feelings were faulty. I didn't recognize the real issues buried deep down. I never poured out my pain because I didn't know that I was wounded. I had no idea that I was riddled with rejection. I was blinded to my own issues. I even considered myself to be a successful Christian woman.

What's Happening Inside?

Think of your emotional infrastructure as being like the plumbing for the kitchen sink. There is a pipe that connects the water tank with the tap. When we turn the tap, water flows from the tank, travels along the pipe and comes rushing out. However, if the tap were disconnected from the pipe, the water in the tank would have no means of escape. At times, as a result of the build up of pressure, there may be an explosive release. Now change the picture slightly. Imagine that your soul is the tank. If your pipe is disconnected, you will not have a healthy means of experiencing or releasing your feelings. They will be trapped inside. Undue pressure may cause a forced release. Any outburst would probably be unpleasant or even destructive.

Torn Apart

Charlotte had a traumatic childhood. Her father left home when she was only three because Charlotte's mother would beat him black and blue. Charlotte's dad left his little girl with the woman who had terrorized him. Day after day, even as a toddler, Charlotte was left at home with only her dog for comfort. She would often weep with her arms wrapped around her pet's neck. Then her dog died. The only living creature that gave her any comfort passed away. There was no longer any point in crying. Charlotte was not taught to use a knife or a fork and would often be forced by her mother to eat her dinner off their dirty floor. As well as experiencing physical abuse and emotional neglect at the hands of the woman who was supposed to take care of her, Charlotte was sexually abused by her grandfather. It was not until she was eleven years of age that Charlotte was placed in a new family.

Disconnected

When she first came to Healed for Life, Charlotte's heart was like Jericho: tightly shut. Although she knew she had suffered terribly, she was completely detached from her feelings. God ministered to some of the hurts she had suffered in adult life. However, true restoration only began when Charlotte made the brave decision to allow the Lord to mend her emotional infrastructure. As we led her in prayer, she apologized to the Lord for shutting down her emotions. She told God that she was willing to feel again. Charlotte started to feel the pain of her past and this became her ticket to restoration. She poured out her heart like water before the face of the Lord and deep healing began.

After attending her second Healed for Life, Charlotte explained: "I could never relate to the little girl who went through all that trauma. It felt like it had happened to somebody else. It was as if I was looking at the life of a nasty little stranger." She looked up and continued as a sweet smile spread across her face. "But now, I know it's me. I experienced her pain and was healed of so much shame. I now feel human. I can feel. Best of all, I am at peace with me." When we can feel, we can be healed.

Sometimes, the Holy Spirit does an instant repair by revealing the truth. The Lord reconnects the pipe and the pain comes out. At other times, it is more of a journey. There are a number of reasons why you may have become disconnected from your feelings. The key to the healing of your soul will probably be hidden in one or more of these places.

1. Pain

You might have suffered terribly at an early age. Perhaps the pain was so overwhelming that it was too difficult to handle. King David understood that sort of agony: "I am ready to fall, and my sorrow is continually before me." (Psalms 38:17). As a result, you distanced yourself from your feelings in order to achieve much needed relief. Either consciously or unconsciously, you detached yourself from the sadness of your soul. Psalm 119:28 says, "My soul melts from heaviness." Sometimes we go through so much that our souls stop functioning. You may have learned ways of separating yourself from feelings of pain, loss and grief. You might have turned off your emotions so that you do not have to feel. God wants to heal your soul.

2. Shame

Someone may have made you feel ashamed of yourself. Perhaps you cried in front of your father. He failed to comfort you - scolding you instead. Maybe you broke down in tears among friends who then mocked you for it. Shame is an unbearable experience which causes us to shun the memory which allowed it into our lives. Shame clings to us: "My dishonor is continually before me, and the shame of my face has covered me." (Psalms 44:15). If you were humiliated or ridiculed, your heart may have connected that unpleasant experience with vulnerability and decided to shut down. The Lord wants to take away every sense of stigma and restore honor to your heart.

3. Lessons

Maybe you were taught not to cry. You might have faced constant comments such as "dry up" or "man up". Perhaps you grew up in a family or a culture where tears were associated with weakness, so you learned to suppress sadness or switch off your emotions. Maybe, despite your deepest desire, no-one listened so you decided that feelings were pointless. Psalm 119:18 says, "My soul breaks with longing..." Several years ago, I visited a massive orphanage in Ghana, West Africa. There was an entire wing for infants under six months of age. I will never forget walking along the long, dark corridor to the deafening sound of silence. It was heartbreaking. Not one of about 50 babies was crying. Why? They must have learned very early in life that weeping was pointless. No-one cared. No-one would come.

If you look back over your life, were you taught somehow that tears were pointless or a sign of weakness? That's a lesson that needs to be unlearned and unraveled. Sometimes we have to repent. Recognizing that you have an inner issue is the first step towards finding the right solution. When we think we are well, we see no need for change and therefore remain the same. Ignorance is not bliss, it is blindness.

If you have been showing soul symptoms like those described above, I would like to pray with you now. Psalm 23:3 says, "He restores my soul." God is the Master Healer who is able to fix any flaw in our feelings. He is able to rewire, renew and reconnect us in our innermost beings.

Heavenly Father,

I bring my heart before you today. I ask You to completely restore my emotions so that they function in the way You intended. I am so sorry for any moment in my life when I deliberately detached myself from my feelings. Please forgive me, oh Lord. I give You permission to open up the floodgates of my emotions. I am willing and ready to feel whatever I need to feel so that my heart can be made whole. I want to be like You: able to experience and express all my emotions effectively.

Holy Spirit, shine Your light deep inside and show me the pain, shame or conditioning that caused me to stop feeling. (If the Lord has revealed a memory, tell Him now exactly what happened. Explain how it hurt you or how it made you

feel ashamed or afraid. Pour out your pain in His presence.)
I ask You to heal my heart. Release Your wonderful love into my innermost being so that I can be made whole.

I thank You so much for Your kindness to me. I love you with all my heart.

In Jesus' name, I pray,

Amen.

4. Vows

If you fall into any of the earlier categories, you will probably have made some sort of vow at one time in your life. Inner vows are most often made in childhood in an effort to avoid pain. In adult life, we tend to make vows that we will never behave in certain ways. You may remember making inner promises or you might have buried the memory. Either way, when we make a vow, it binds us. Numbers 30:2 says, "If a man makes a vow... or swears an oath to bind himself... he shall do according to all that proceeds out of his mouth."

Shut Down

Brian was playing in the kitchen with his brother. His father had always warned him not to touch the oven, but curiosity overcame him. Reaching up on his tiptoes, he placed the palm of his hand flat upon the hob and then screamed. He snatched his hand away, but the damage was done. His father came running to the war zone. Brian was crying his little heart out and was desperate for reassurance. Instead, Brian's dad scolded him for disobedience.

There was something about that experience that caused Brian to shut down. He vowed that he would never allow anyone to see him cry again and believed that he was stronger because of this decision. He associated tears with weakness and was prone to judge others for any level of emotionalism. We need to realize that God has given us a release mechanism called tears for a purpose. Brian had a host of inner issues that needed healing, but he would never allow himself to face the pain because of his vow.

I prayed for this young man because I could see deep wounds being held to ransom by strong resistance. The Lord gave me a word of knowledge. I asked Brian if he had been burnt as a little boy. He broke and fell to the ground weeping. He then shared how he had vowed to remain emotionally constrained. This was the breakthrough needed for the healing of his soul.

Unlocking The Door

When we vow, we lock ourselves into certain behavior with our words. To make matters worse, a vow often originates from judgement. We judge an abuser to be evil, so we vow that we will never trust a man again. We judge our parents' marriage to be a disaster, so we vow never to marry. We judge a family member to be a failure, so we vow that we will never be out of work. We judge our ex to be a disgrace, so we vow never to love again. We judge our father to be cruel, so we vow never to let anyone hurt us again.

Matthew 7:1 (NIV) says, "Do not judge, or you too will be judged." You and I need God's mercy every time we mess up. If we hold judgements, we open the door to others judging us every time we miss the mark. We need to rid ourselves of judgment for the sake of our future. Vows are dangerous. We bind ourselves with our own words. We need to repent for the judgement and renounce the vows. Let us pray right away. If you remember vows you made, tell God what they were. If you don't know if you made any inner promises, pray with me generally.

Heavenly Father,

I am so sorry for any vows that I may have made either in childhood or in adult life. I realize that I may have bound myself with my own words. Forgive me, oh Lord. **(If you remember specific vows, tell the Lord now by saying:)** *I am sorry for the vow I made when...* **(tell the Lord exactly what happened and what you vowed).** *I break that vow in the name of Jesus and I ask for Your forgiveness. I am so sorry for judging those who hurt me. Your word tells me not to judge so I ask for Your forgiveness.* **(Now repeat that prayer until you have dealt with all vows you remember making.)**

I declare that I am free from every inner vow that bound me.

In the name of Jesus, I pray,

Amen.

Your Mind

Your mind was created to process thoughts, file and retrieve memories, to reason and to imagine. You are probably aware of disorders which can occur when our minds are not functioning properly. However, I want to deal with one area where we may put our limitations down to personal deficiency rather than a wounded soul. Let's look at the whole notion of creativity.

Right at the beginning of the Bible we see God's extravagant imagination on display. Out of nothing, He created the sun, moon and stars as well as mountains, rivers, woods, oceans, deserts and every living creature. He is an awesome God with an extraordinary imagination. He is exceptionally creative, and you and I are made in His image. All too often, I hear people say that they are not creative. If that's your view of yourself, I would like to challenge your perceptions. You are made in the image of the most creative One ever to have lived. The abilities to imagine and create are core functions of the mind.

Broken Imagination

Rita loved art as a child. One day, when she was eight, she was asked to present her drawing in school. Full of joy, she walked to the front with her picture. Instead of praise, Rita was ridiculed in front of the whole class. Her teacher mocked her efforts, saying: "This is rubbish. There is no hope for you. You would need to go to an entire university of drawing before you could even try your hand at art!" Rita returned to her seat feeling ashamed and humiliated. Those words pierced her heart but also molded her view of herself. That day, Rita unconsciously concluded something like this: "I might be clever, but I'm not creative. I can add but I can't draw." These inner beliefs stayed with Rita throughout her schooling and early adult life. When she had to choose subjects to study, despite her love for biology, she excluded herself on the basis that she could not draw diagrams. Even in her relationship with God, she never saw pictures when she prayed and was only able to hear God through His word.

Rita came to Healed for Life. As I ministered, the Holy Spirit shone His light into her heart. The Lord took her back to that painful day at school and she wept in His presence. She realized for the first time that her opinion of herself was based on trauma rather than the truth. God is creative, and she was made in His image. The Lord healed her mind. Since then, Rita has enjoyed her new-found creativity. It does not stop there, though. Since her healing, her imagination has been unleashed and she hears and sees in the Spirit like never before.

What About You?

Maybe you are like that dear lady. You have always seen yourself as lacking imagination or creativity. Maybe God is speaking to you about another aspect of the mind of God. I don't believe we should accept any limitations. I remember when I apologized to the Lord for constantly saying that I was not technical. Instead, I asked the Holy Spirit for His help. If you realize that words spoken over you have made you believe that you are not creative, or bad at math, or generally not very clever, it is time to allow the Lord to heal your mind. Let's pray.

Heavenly Father,

Thank You that I am made in Your wonderful image. You are creative, You are mathematical, You are infinitely able. I am so sorry for any limitations I have placed upon myself. Please forgive me, Lord. (If you remember something that happened or words that were spoken that wounded you, tell the Lord what you experienced right now. Explain how you felt and pour out your heart like water before Him. Be as specific as possible.) Heal my soul deep down, I pray, oh Lord.

Now Lord, I want to thank You that I am made in Your image. I am creative, I am able, I have the mind of Christ. I can process thoughts effectively and my memory is blessed.

I give You all the praise and glory!

In Jesus' name, I pray,

Amen.

Your Will

Your will enables you to make choices and decisions. It controls your voluntary actions. Occasionally, the things that we have suffered can lead to a broken will. This is much less common than wounds to our emotions or mind. However, when the will is damaged it can adversely affect our lives. If you grew up in a home where your father, mother or caretaker was excessively controlling, it might have damaged your ability to make decisions or choices. If you were subjected to any form of domestic violence or abuse that meant your voluntary actions were controlled by someone else, this could have broken your will. God wants to heal you of the trauma you suffered and restore your ability to make decisions. This might be the first time that you are realizing why you have struggled in life. Allow the Lord to take you on a journey to wholeness. If you have struggled a great deal in this area, the spirit of control may have had a part to play in your oppression. We will ask God to heal your heart and then we will deal with any spiritual opposition. Let's pray.

Heavenly Father,

I am so grateful that You have given me an effective will. I now realize that it must have been damaged somewhere along the way, so I ask You to heal me deep within. (If you now remember being subjected to sustained control, tell the Lord exactly what happened and how it made you feel. Pour out your heart like water before Him.) Father, I ask You to make my heart whole and mend my broken will.

Now I forgive those who hurt me in this area and I renounce control and cut it out of my life. I take authority over the spirit of control that has oppressed me. In the name of Jesus,

I drive out every spirit trying to control me. I declare that I am free!

I give You all the praise and glory. I thank You that You will never force me to do anything. Thank You that You gave me free will as a gift. Thank You that You trust me to be able to make good decisions. I choose also to trust myself to make right choices, with Your help.

Thank You for Your love.

In Jesus' name, I pray,

Amen.

Chapter 4
YOUR SPIRIT

Several years ago, a prophet gave me a word. It was short but curious. It left me questioning some of my long-held beliefs. The woman of God declared, "The Lord has made you an apostolic healer. You will bring healing to many - body, soul and spirit." God has used me for years to bring healing to the hearts of His people. I have also seen many physical miracles. At Healed for Life we find that many are set free from long term physical illnesses. As their hearts are healed, diseases leave! We have seen restoration of skin conditions, blood disorders, heart problems, stroke symptoms, joint pains and much more. The part of the word that puzzled me was the notion that I would bring healing to people's spirits. I had always believed that from the moment of salvation, the human spirit was brought to fullness of life. This word put my doctrine in question. I did a Genesis to Revelation study of the human spirit and was amazed at what I learned.

Uncovering the Truth

Just as the soul (and of course the body) can be wounded, defiled or broken, so the human spirit can be damaged. For years, I believed that our souls needed to be restored but that our spirits were immune to infection. However, that is not what the Bible teaches. 1 Thessalonians 5:23 says, "Now may the God of peace Himself sanctify you completely; and may your whole spirit, soul, and body be preserved blameless at the coming of our Lord Jesus Christ." Why would our spirits need to be sanctified or preserved if they were instantly perfected at salvation? The reason that our spirits need to be made blameless is because, just like our souls and our bodies, they are fallible. Jesus challenged his disciples in Luke 9:55, saying: "You do not know what manner of spirit you are of..." There is no suggestion that He believed His disciples were demonized. I believe He was questioning the sanctity of their spirits. Paul the Apostle wrote that fellow Christians had refreshed both his spirit and the spirit of Titus in 1 Corinthians 16:18 and 2 Corinthians 7:13. If their spirits were refreshed, they must surely have been weary? Even Jesus *became* strong in spirit (Luke 2:40), showing the changing nature of the human spirit.

Our spirits come from God. The start of your life was not your birth, it was the moment your spirit came alive. Salvation was your rebirth, the time your spirit was awakened to eternal life. The Hebrew for spirit is *ruah* and it means wind, breath or to blow. Job 32:8 says, "There is a spirit in man, the breath of the Almighty." At salvation, God's Spirit breathes life into us, we are born again and come to new life. His perfect Spirit lives and remains in us. His Spirit is *never* defiled. It is our human spirit that may need sanctifying, preserving and refreshing.

The Human Spirit

I was staggered when I started to study the human spirit in Scripture. Far from perfection, our spirits can fall prey to a vast array of problems. The Bible teaches that we can have an anxious spirit (Daniel 2:3), a sorrowful spirit (1 Samuel 1:15), an unfaithful spirit (Psalm 78:8), a sullen spirit (1Kings 21:5) and a haughty spirit (Proverbs 16:18) - to mention just a few. Our spirits can be troubled (John 13:21), they can faint, they can be overwhelmed (Psalm 142:3) and be provoked (Acts 17:16).

Just like your soul and body, your spirit may need to be restored and sanctified. There was a lady who attended our church many years ago. She was gifted, committed and passionate. Yet there was something that was always out of balance. There is no doubt that she loved the Lord and hungered after His presence. However, I would often hear negative reports about her, such as: "She railroaded my decisions" or "She forced her way into my life" or "I find her domineering". If I am honest, I too occasionally contended with intimidation when she was around. One day, I spoke to my husband about this lady. I wanted to help her if I could and to protect others. His response was immediate: "She is full of her own spirit."

Full Of Self

Even though I didn't understand back then what my husband was saying doctrinally, it made perfect sense. When this woman walked in the room, you would know that she had arrived. She was determined to fulfill her dreams and pursued them relentlessly, almost irrespective of how her behavior affected others. Ezekiel 13:3 speaks of "...those who follow their own spirit..." Job's 'so called' friend Elihu said, "I am full of words; the spirit within me compels me." (Job 32:18). We know it was not the Holy Spirit pushing him to speak. It must have been his own spirit, bursting with its own ideas. Most of what Elihu said was based on truth. It was how and when he said it that was horribly wrong. He had knowledge without sensitivity to God's Spirit. This is a subtle yet serious issue.

Keeping My Spirit Contrite

If the story we have just heard describes an extreme case of someone who was full of their own spirit, what are the subtle traits that we all need to guard against? I believe the answer is hidden in the second half of a verse we already read: "...the spirit within me compels me." (Job 32:18) When our desire to fulfill our own goals and dreams becomes so compelling that little else matters, we need to watch out. A foundational gospel principle is this: "Most assuredly, I say to you, unless a grain of wheat falls to the ground and dies, it remains alone, but if it dies, it produces much grain." (John 12:24). Death to our desires and dreams is part of the process of growth. If I am completely consumed with my own vision, there is a chance that my spirit is growing unruly. Surrendering to the Holy Spirit often requires sacrifice. Being a faithful servant to someone else's mission helps keep us in check.

Good Stuff!

There are many wonderful attributes that we can develop, including a faithful spirit (Proverbs 11:13), a steadfast spirit (Psalm 51:10), a diligent spirit (Psalm 77:6), a humble spirit (Proverbs 16:19), a calm spirit (Proverbs 17:27), a contrite spirit (Isaiah 57:16) and a strong spirit (Luke 1:80). Of course, many of these are also fruits of the Holy Spirit. The more we surrender to His ways and are filled with His love, the more we can overflow with His goodness and humility.

When It Breaks

One of the first things that struck me when I studied this subject in Scripture was the realization that the human spirit can break. Remember, words often have two or more meanings. I am not referring to the "broken and contrite spirit" that David talked about in Psalm 51. That was clearly a reference to a deep inner repentance and humility. This is different. The Bible teaches that our human spirit can be wounded and broken. Of course, if your spirit is fractured, it will not fulfill its purpose and you will struggle. Let's have a look at what the Bible teaches. As well as being our source of life, we learn that there are three important purposes for your spirit.

1. Communication

If you want to speak to a friend in another location, you use a telephone. If you want to chat to someone in the same room, you use your voice. You communicate with the Lord by your spirit. My spirit is my online connection with God. It is also the means by which we fellowship. You probably know the famous prayer taken from 2 Corinthians 13:14: "May the grace of the Lord Jesus Christ, and the love of God, and the fellowship of the Holy Spirit be with you all." Fellowship is a Greek word *koinōnia*, which means communion or partnership. It refers to a tremendously close connection between God and man. The bond of fellowship is formed when our spirit connects with His Spirit.

If your spirit is broken, you may watch people worship God and wonder why they look so captivated. Despite loving the Lord and telling Him as much, you might not enjoy an emotional connection with Him. You may see tears stream down faces filled with joy while you have a much less rewarding experience. John 4:24 tells us that "God is Spirit and those who worship Him must worship in spirit..." If you struggle to connect in personal praise, it may be that your spirit is wounded or broken. It is not that God loves you less. It is not that you are a less loving person. It is probably because your spirit needs to be restored. If the telephone mast is knocked down in a storm, you will be unable to make or receive calls. Electricians must repair the pylon so that you can connect again. In the same way, there are certain types of storms that can damage our spirits. We will look at these in a little while. But for now, I just want you to realize that you may well need the Lord to repair your spirit.

2. Identity

Knowing deep down that God is your loving Heavenly Father creates a sense of identity. Understanding that we are children of the Most High instills a sense of belonging in our hearts. He could have chosen to be your boss or commanding officer. However, your loving Lord chose to receive you as His child. Even before my heart was healed, I always had a strong sense of God as my Father. This anchored my soul. I was full of issues, but I was somehow grounded. Romans 8:16 explains *how* we can know on the inside that He is our Father. Let us read it in the Amplified: "The Spirit Himself [thus] testifies together with our own spirit, [assuring us] that we are children of God. " The Spirit Himself assures us of our identity and value by testifying to *our spirit* that we are children of God. It is in our very core that we know that we are God's children. One of the most important functions of the human spirit is that it can bear witness to the fact that we are loved by our Heavenly Father. If you struggle to experience God as your Father, you may have a broken spirit.

3. Transformation

Your spirit is also God's window into your secret world. Proverbs 20:20 says, "The spirit of a man is the lamp of the Lord, searching all the inner depths of his heart." Our human spirit provides a torch for the Holy Spirit to search our hearts. You are already at chapter four of this book so by now you will know how important the condition of your heart is to your future. We get hurt on our journey through life. We get dry and discouraged. God never wants to treat our symptoms alone. He always seeks to deal with causes. My spirit is the window that God shines His light through to reveal the issues in my heart that He knows I need to face. If your spirit is broken, it will probably be hard to connect with your memories. That might mean that you have only very sparse recollections or it could be that you see the pictures of what happened but no sense that you were actually there. Even in times of prayer, when others are able to remember the pain of the past, you feel detached.

What Breaks the Human Spirit?

There are varying degrees of functionality in a person's spirit. You may discover that your spirit is in communication with God but not working fully. On the other hand, you may realize that it is completely broken. Perhaps you are somewhere in between. Wherever you are on this spectrum, the good news is that you can be healed. The Bible reveals three reasons why the human spirit might be broken.

1. Sorrow Upon Sorrow

Sadly, terrible things happen to good people. We all experience pain in our lives. However, there are some stories I hear of sorrow upon sorrow. One tragedy followed by another. Brutal rejection then cruel abandonment. Excruciating pain that would be too much for anyone to manage. Proverbs 15:13 says: "...by sorrow of the heart the spirit is broken." If your childhood was a catalogue of cruel calamities, I am sure that your heart was broken. Furthermore, you may discover that your spirit was deeply wounded. The New Living Translation puts that verse like this: "... a broken heart crushes the spirit." I believe this expresses the meaning perfectly. Sometimes the pain of your life can be so intense that it squeezes the very life out of your spirit. Psalm 143:3-4 says: "For the enemy has persecuted my soul; he has crushed my life to the ground... Therefore, my spirit is overwhelmed within me; my heart within me is distressed." In Hebrew the word for overwhelmed actually means fainted. When the circumstances of life are terribly tough, the distress can be unbearable. It can crush the very life out of you and even cause your spirit to faint.

You may have wondered why others were healed while you walked away from meetings still hurting. If your spirit was broken by pain, you will probably need restoration for it before you can receive all the healing your heart needs. Because your spirit is God's torch that He uses to reveal hidden pain in the recesses of your heart, getting your spirit fixed first will help.

2. Wicked, Wounding Words

Proverbs 15:4 says, "A wholesome tongue is a tree of life, but perverseness in it breaks the spirit." There is a stark contrast. Words can bring life and affirmation. However, at the same time they can damage the spirit. The New International Version puts the verse like this: "The soothing tongue is a tree of life, but a perverse tongue crushes the spirit." The word perverse means to go counter to what is expected. It is perverse when parents who were supposed to protect you instead cruelly pull you apart with their words. It is perverse when family members who are expected to build you up in fact tear you down.

We have all been on the receiving end of cutting comments. We have all been wounded by words. Nonetheless, there is something especially crushing when words are knowingly used as weapons by those deemed to be your nearest and dearest. Proverbs 12:18 says, "There is one who speaks like the piercings of a sword." Maybe things were said to you that cut through to your core. It is not just what they said but how they said it and who heard. The Bible calls wounding words fiery darts. They come like arrows and cut us to pieces. Maybe your dad repeatedly tore you apart - even in front of friends. Perhaps your spouse stabbed you with constant cruel comments. They humiliated you with rude remarks that left you reeling in pain. When that keeps happening, it can reach the point when something eventually snaps on the inside. Sometimes there is one piercing that is fatal and the spirit breaks. Whether you have been mortally wounded on the inside by constant cruel comments or you realize that you still have some darts in your heart, help is at hand. God is able to remove the arrows, heal the wounds and renew your spirit.

3. When You Think God is Against You

Scripture calls the devil the father of lies. Everything he says is either totally untrue or a perversion of the truth. Satan seeks to separate you from God and from your destiny. He is the author of all confusion, chaos and pain. In contrast, God is good. James 1:17 explains that "Every good gift and every perfect gift is from above, and comes down from the Father of lights, with whom there is no variation or shadow of turning." This is confirming that there is no darkness whatsoever in God. Everything good comes down from above while everything bad originates below. One demonic lie that can be extremely destructive is that God is responsible for your pain and suffering.

Hope is an anchor. It is the belief that God is foundational for a bright future. If we think that God is the author of heartbreaking sorrow, it can break our spirit. Job in the Bible lost everything. His children were killed by a freak accident, his business was destroyed, and he became terribly sick. That would have been hard enough to handle. However, what made matters much worse was that Job believed that God was his problem. Deep in his heart, he supposed his suffering was the doing of the Lord: "For the arrows of the Almighty are within me; my spirit drinks in their poison; the terrors of God are arrayed against me." (Job 6:4). When we believe that God is against us, it is like drinking poison. Job, who once knew sweet fellowship with his Heavenly Father, now felt like the object of His hatred: "He has shattered me; He also has taken me by the neck and shaken me to pieces; He has set me up for His target." (Job 17:12). What broke Job's spirit was the false belief that God was the one behind his suffering. At that point, he lost all hope: "My spirit is broken, my days are extinguished, the grave is ready for me." (Job 17:1).

When we have a broken spirit, it can feel as though all is lost. Hope is gone. All sense of purpose is extinguished like a smoldering wick. If you realize that you have believed that God is against you, I want to assure you that your loving Heavenly Father has only good in store. Isaiah 42:3 promises that "A bruised reed He will not break, and a dimly burning wick He will not quench..." He is for you and He is ready to help.

The Restorer

God is not only your Designer but also your Healer. He can fix any flaws or breakages in your body and soul. He is also able to restore your spirit. Isaiah 57:15 says that God will "...revive the spirit of the humble." The Hebrew word for revive is *ḥâyâ* and it means to quicken, to nourish, to recover, to repair, to restore and to make alive. The word for humble in the Hebrew is *šâp□âl* and it literally means depressed. If you feel like life has been dwindling on the inside and that heaviness has been covering you like a cloak, God wants to breathe new life into your innermost being. He is ready to renew your spirit and lift you out of depression. He can repair damage and He can heal a completely broken spirit. Irrespective of where you are on the spectrum, God can restore and revive your spirit! He can breathe life deep within.

King David asked God to renew his spirit after he messed his life up in Psalm 51. The word renew means to rebuild, repair and make new. Ezekiel 11:19b says, "I will put a new spirit within them..." Even if you need a brand-new start, God is able! As you are renewed, you will be able to enjoy your Heavenly Father, sweet fellowship with the Spirit, wonderful worship and divine access to your memory bank. Restoration starts by going to the root of the issue.

A New Start

As you have read, you have probably identified with one or more of the biblical causes of a broken spirit. Perhaps you have been overwhelmed with sorrow in your life. One sadness after another may have subdued or even suffocated your spirit. It could be that cruel and crushing comments caused something on the inside to die. Maybe you are like Job. Life has thrown you far too many heartbreaking difficulties and disappointments. Somewhere along the way, you ended up believing that God was the author of your sadness and suffering. Even if just one of these applies to you only slightly, let's bring it to God in prayer.

We will first ask the Holy Spirit to heal the pain that caused your spirit to choke or break. Then we will ask God to breathe new life into your innermost being. Below there are two types of prayers. The first is for those of you who have clearly been damaged. The second is for those of you who have a functioning spirit, but you want to be refreshed and renewed.

Restore My Spirit

Heavenly Father,

Thank You that You designed me. You formed me and You know me completely. I am so glad that You are able and willing to restore every broken place in me.

I realize now that my spirit is probably broken. (Now tell God in as much detail as possible what you struggle with as a result of a wounded spirit: communication, worship, fellowship or fathering.) It has been so hard to watch others thrive while I have felt dry. I ask You to mend my spirit today, oh Lord.

I am willing to go back in prayer to the place where things fell apart. (Now tell God how you suffered. If one heartbreak after another suffocated the very life out of you, tell Him. Explain the things that hurt the most and the one or two memories that stand out. Tell God what happened and how it all made you feel. If words were spoken that crushed your spirit, tell the Lord exactly what was said, who said it and how it made you feel. He knows anyway and can handle hearing even crude language if it will help you heal.) Heal my wounded spirit, oh Lord. Pour out your unconditional love afresh and restore what was broken.

(If you believed the lie that God was your problem, let me lead you now:) Lord, I am so sorry for believing You were my problem. I now realize that this was a lie from the pit of hell. You love me. You are for me and You are always good. I attributed evil to You even though You are always righteous. I am so sorry. Forgive me, oh Lord. I realize that the enemy is to blame. The devil is the author of all my agony. I thank You Lord that the plans that You have for me are good. You want the very best for me. I place my trust in You again because You are always faithful. I will daily say out loud that You are my loving Heavenly Father.

Now, Lord, revive my spirit according to Your word! Renew, rebuild and restore my spirit. Breathe new life into my life today, I pray. Revive me. I receive fresh breath from heaven into my innermost being. Thank You for a brand-new connection between Your Spirit and my spirit. Fellowshipping with You will become my new norm. I open up the deep places of my heart for You to reveal any pains that You want to heal. Thank You Lord God that You are my Father. You are my Daddy-God. I am Your well-loved child.

I give You all the glory for the new work that You have started in me today.

In Jesus' name, I pray,

Amen.

Renew My Spirit

Heavenly Father,

I desire for my spirit to constantly bring glory to You. Examine me and try me. If there is any wound or kink in my spirit, Lord show me now, I pray. If I have been full of my own spirit, forgive me, oh Lord. I surrender, and I submit to the work of Your Spirit. Teach me once again to die daily and to be a servant.

If there is any damage - by words or sorrow or even from believing a lie - shine Your light deep down and reveal to me so that I can surrender it to you. **(If the Lord has reminded you of any hurtful experience or wounding words, tell Him what happened, what was said and how it made you feel. Pour out your heart in His presence.)** Heal me, I pray. Take away all angst and sorrow and remove any fiery dart from my heart. I surrender to Your love.

(If you have believed the lie that God is your problem, pray this prayer:) Lord, I am so sorry for believing You were my problem. I now realize that this was a foul lie from the pit of hell. You love me. You are for me and You are always good. I attributed evil to You, even though You are always righteous. I am so sorry. Forgive me, oh Lord. I realize that the enemy is to blame. The devil is the author of all my agonies. I thank You Lord that the plans that You have for me are good. You want the very best for me. I place my trust in You again because You are always faithful.

Now Lord, revive my spirit according to Your word! Rebuild and restore me. Breathe new life into my life today, I pray. I receive fresh breath from heaven into my innermost being. May I have a faithful, steadfast, strong and humble spirit, oh Lord.

In Jesus' name, I pray,

Amen.

Chapter 5
ARE YOU AN INTERNALIZER?

Do you often find yourself feeling dry or discouraged? Do you ever have a sense of heaviness that won't shift? Do you feel a sadness beneath the surface? Our emotions were designed to be felt and expressed. When they are trapped on the inside or buried deep within, our souls can stagnate. Remember the picture we painted in chapter one of our hearts like vast vaults, with countless filing cabinets holding multitudes of folders? When we subdue our emotions, we push them into the vault and shut the door. Imagine every corner filled to overflowing with junk. It would be disheartening to look inside. No wonder we find ourselves weighed down. The devil is always looking for ways to derail your destiny. He knows that a blocked soul is a sure way to get you to slow down. Or even better, to make you stop altogether.

We sometimes think that the Lord is a little detached emotionally. That is entirely untrue. We see Him exhibiting a vast array of emotions throughout the Bible. Our Maker showed sadness (Jeremiah 8:18), regret (1 Samuel 15:11), anger (Isaiah 30:27), grief (Judges 10:16), joy (Zephaniah 3:17), love (John 3:16), hate (Psalm 45:7), rejection (Matthew 27:46) and so much more in Scripture. He both feels and expresses freely. The Lord felt the agony of regret as He watched His dear son King Saul become more preoccupied with people's opinions than pleasing his Maker. Jesus spoke about the heartbreak of rejection by friends, leaders, and even His Father in heaven. We are made in the image of God. We were designed to feel and express just like our Maker.

Nearly all of us internalize at one time or another. Some people constantly bottle up their real feelings while others just do it occasionally. However, I do believe the majority of us sweep our stuff under the proverbial carpet on a fairly regular basis. There are a number of reasons why we do this.

1. We Are Unaware

Sometimes we don't know what is going on inside. Jeremiah 17:9 in the Amplified says: "The heart is deceitful above all things... Who can know it [perceive, understand, be acquainted with his own heart and mind]?" This verse explains that our hearts are almost unfathomable and that they can lie to us. This is one of the reasons why God sent prophets. The purpose of one of Daniel's missions was to help a man understand the hidden secrets of his own heart. Centuries later, Jesus came partly "...that the thoughts of many hearts may be revealed" (Luke 2:35). Throughout His earthly ministry, Jesus looked beyond the way things appeared and pinpointed the real issues that folk were battling with on the inside. If you will invite Him, the Holy Spirit will open the vault and show you the pain that you unwittingly locked away. He will uncover the buried hurts that have been holding you back. He will reveal it because when you feel it, He can heal it.

2. It Is Too Uncomfortable

All too often, we don't express our emotions because the feelings in our hearts are too uncomfortable. We somehow convince ourselves that if we ignore them, they will go away. I wish that were true, but it is pure fiction. If we ignore unwanted issues, they simply sink to the bottom of our souls. They clutter our hearts and weigh us down. Proverbs 20:20 says, "The spirit of man is the lamp of the Lord searching the inner depths of the heart." He highlights discomfort because He wants us to deal with our difficulties and enjoy the freedom of healing.

Humiliation

During the launch of one of my books, my publisher set up a short book tour for me in the North Carolina mountains. It involved speaking at a small conference of about 300 people, doing a book signing and conducting some television interviews. I am not comfortable driving on the right-hand side of the road (in Britain we drive on the left) so a kind couple from Miami, Florida, offered to help. They flew to Atlanta to meet me. I rented a car and they drove me to the venue. I booked two hotel rooms for the two nights we would be in the area.

When I walked into the conference venue, I was stunned. There were 300 seats, for sure. However, and I'm not exaggerating, there were only seven people in attendance and I had brought two of them! My head started to spin. The anticipated book sales were supposed to go some way towards covering the hotel bill and car hire. But that wasn't the worst of it. I just felt so embarrassed. Shame is a very uncomfortable feeling, so we normally push it down inside and pretend we are fine. We may express agitation or anger, but we rarely show it when we feel a fool. Often the reason we internalize our emotions is that what we really feel is too uncomfortable. It is easier to ignore it than to face the unpalatable truth.

Behind Closed Doors

Back to North Carolina. I preached that first night with all of my heart. I had promised the Lord a long time ago that I would always give my best, whether I was ministering to ten or ten thousand. As soon as we arrived back at the hotel, I closed my door and dropped to my knees. I poured out my heart before God. "Lord, this is not what they promised. I feel so stupid. I am so embarrassed. My new friends drove all this way just for this. I feel humiliated and ashamed of myself." I wept as I prayed for a few minutes. When I got up from the floor, I was at peace again. The embarrassment was gone because I had expressed it in His presence. The churning had lifted because I had given my disappointment to God.

I had to return the following day to continue with the conference. I was able to walk in love towards the handful of attendees because my heart was healed. I was able to be gracious to our host because the awkward embarrassment was gone. Of the seven people who attended that conference, three are now working with me at Healed for Life. If I had not known how to pour out my heart in private, I would not have behaved honorably in public. If I had not acted with integrity in front of others, I do not believe that they would be with me today. When we deal with our most uncomfortable emotions, we are able to be our best - even in the worst circumstances.

3. Out Of Practice

Perhaps your soul has been silenced for so long that you have forgotten what it is like to feel. You will need to make daily decisions to let your heart feel. Then, when emotions emerge on the inside, make sure you go to a private place and express yourself in prayer. Bit by bit, as you allow your newly discovered feelings out, you will start to create healthy emotional habits.

What Is Internalization?

My definition of internalization is not allowing emotions or feelings to show, even though you think about them. Of course, it is vital that we learn to manage our emotions. Proverbs 25:28 says, "A man who has no rule over his own spirit is like a city broken down without walls." We need to know how to take charge of our feelings. However, that is completely different to suppressing our emotions. When we feel, it is a physical experience at our core, in our gut or in our belly. That is how we were designed from the start. In the Garden of Eden, Adam and Eve will have experienced joy, excitement, peace, wonder, amazement, love and so much more! They were fully alive - body, soul and spirit.

When the fall came, a whole host of new emotions will have flooded their souls. All too soon, they felt the weight of shame and guilt, then the heaviness of sadness and disappointment. I am sure they were angry and frustrated. Following closely behind, no doubt they knew the vacuum of loneliness and deep regret. Perhaps even depression entered in. I don't know anyone who enjoys negative emotion so the temptation even from the start will have been to separate themselves from those feelings and bury them deep down. I believe that countless generations before us have perfected the dark art of internalization.

The Power of Pouring

The Psalmists are known for their powerful outpourings of emotion in the presence of God. Yet even one of these worshippers wanted to push their feelings down: "Unless the Lord had been my help, my soul would have settled in silence." (Psalm 94:17). We need to understand that it is not the will of God for us to hold our hurts and pains inside. There is research that shows a correlation between dementia and the suppression of emotion. Of course, that is not the cause in every case, but some link does make sense. If we practice detachment from reality by not acknowledging our true inner state, then we may unwittingly open the door to more serious problems in the future.

Job in the Bible suffered terribly. He lost his family, his livelihood and even his health. He was obviously desperate to push away the pain and pretend all was well: "I will forget my complaint, I will put off my sad face and wear a smile" (Job 9:27). However, in the midst of his grief, he began to understand that we can experience a sense of relief when we express ourselves: "If I remain silent, how am I eased?" (Job 16:6b). King David went a step further and said that internalization only amplified his issues and damaged his health: "When I kept silent, my bones grew old..." (Psalm 32:3).

Blocked Springs

Your heart is meant to be a spring of living water. John 7:38 says, "He who believes in Me, as the Scripture has said, out of his heart will flow rivers of living water." Your soul should flow with love, joy and peace. However, if we are holding our thoughts and bottling our feelings, our souls will stagnate and be more like a swamp than a spring. It is easy to think that this is a personality issue and that the way we are is just 'the way we are'. Some people gush, and others hold back. However, if our habits are bad for our health then we need to ask God to do a work on the inside so that we can live a fulfilling and rewarding life.

The Damage That Can Be Done

Every story in Scripture is included for our instruction. The lives of men and women have been laid bare in the Bible so that we can learn and grow. Sometimes we need to dig beneath the surface to discover why God put these people's private struggles on paper for eternity. If you will open your heart, I believe God will speak to you through one young woman's sad story.

Tamar was King David's daughter. She was a princess with a bright future. All too often, horrible things happen to good people. I think that is because the devil detests nice people. Well, something terrible happened to this young lady. Tamar's half brother Amnon had an all-consuming crush on her and hatched a plan to trick Tamar into his bedroom. This young woman will have trusted her brother. She could not have anticipated what was about to happen. Amnon sent everyone away so that he could be alone with his sister. Then he forced her to have sex with him. Tamar pleaded with her brother to stop. No amount of anguish or arguing would deter him. Amnon raped Tamar.

There are some "suddenlies" that we long for: a promotion or a debt cancellation, perhaps. However, there are other "suddenlies" that are soul-destroying. In one horrific attack, Tamar's life changed forever. She was brutally betrayed by the brother she was hoping to help back to health. She was robbed of her innocence. Things then got even worse. Probably disgusted with himself and with her as a constant reminder of what he'd done, Amnon threw his sister out of his house. Tamar felt ashamed, rejected and heartbroken. She ran from Amnon's house in floods of bitter tears. Traumatized and terrified, she turned to another brother, Absalom.

The Power Of Tears

God gave us a powerful release mechanism called crying. When we weep, we offload sorrow and sadness. King David, one of the Bible's greatest heroes and strongest leaders, cried regularly: "... All night I make my bed swim; I drench my couch with my tears." (Psalms 6:6). Joseph wept many times: so loudly that the neighbors heard and so long that he stained his cheeks red. Joseph cried in the arms of his father and as he embraced his brothers. Jeremiah spoke of his tears before the Lord and encouraged the people of Israel to cry. Jesus wept, and Paul sobbed. These healthy role models knew how to release sadness and give their pain to God. Crying occasionally is normal and healthy.

Tamar was doing the only thing that she could do at that time. She was weeping. There is no doubt that it was the right thing to do. If she had only continued - following in her father David's footsteps and telling the Lord about every agony and the pain within - I believe God would have healed her heart. Absalom did not know how to help his sister. He loved her, but he could not assist. Instead of sitting down with Tamar, listening to her anguish and speaking kindly to her, Absalom said: "But now hold your peace, my sister. He is your brother; do not take this thing to heart." This was horribly wrong for three reasons.

First, Absalom told Tamar to hold her peace. Tamar was traumatized. There was no peace to hold. Second, Absalom suggested his sister should ignore the issue because the perpetrator was her brother. Many people have a deep sense of loyalty that makes them think that they must protect family privacy at all costs. If you have been hurt by your nearest and dearest, the Lord wants to heal you. It is not dishonoring to admit to God that you were wounded by your relatives. In fact, it is essential that you are honest with God and ask Him to heal you. Absalom's third statement was ridiculous. Tamar was broken. This brutal attack had torn her apart. Yet her brother advised her not to take this matter to heart. He was implying that she should stop crying and push down her pain. He told her to internalize her hurt. Perhaps he could not handle the agony of seeing his sister in pain. Maybe he thought that showing sadness was a sign of weakness. It could be that he believed tears would give Amnon another victory. The very next phrase is so sad. " So, Tamar remained desolate." (2 Samuel 13:20b).

Shut Down

Tamar shut down on the inside. She shut the world out and she shut her mouth. Then she remained desolate for the rest of her life. Sweeping sadness under the carpet does not make it go away. Ignoring disappointment does not bring relief. It settles in our souls, opening the door to dryness and discouragement. Society often tells us to hide our emotions. Culture teaches us that silence is strength and that emotional detachment from our distress is a sign of maturity. It can be difficult to talk about our pain to God, but the rewards are lasting relief and freedom.

God has a great plan for your life - to prosper you and give you a bright, fulfilling future. It is important that you know this. However, the devil has a plan too. According to John 10:10, satan wants to steal, kill and destroy. He knows he can't just waltz in and end all our lives. So, he tries to spoil them. Satan seeks to destroy your destiny. He knows that your heart determines the course of your life, so he will do everything in his power to keep you constrained by hidden issues.

One of his most dangerous lies is to convince us that we are fine when we are only *partially* healed. The Lord wants to bring us to a place of complete security. He wants us to enjoy enduring inner peace. That only comes as we allow God to highlight hidden hurts and reveal buried insecurities so that He can heal. He wants to take us on a journey to wholeness. He does not want us to stop until our hearts are *really* healed.

Releasing Trapped Words

The Bible tells us to share our innermost issues with the Lord in prayer: "Pour out your heart like water before the face of the Lord." Lamentations 2:19b. When we pour out our heart to a friend, we tell them what has been weighing us down. We share our secrets. That is what we need to do with God. When we tell Him what happened to us and how much it hurt, it helps unlock buried pain. As we speak the words we never said (because we felt we couldn't), we release healing tears in the presence of God. When we tell God how disappointed we really feel, we give Him access to our hearts. He can then reach into the depths of our souls, take away our pain and release His healing love.

I don't know what you have been through. Maybe you were rejected by someone you loved. Perhaps you have suffered humiliating put-downs at work. It could be that you were betrayed by your dearest confidante. It does not matter how big or small the issue. God wants you to be free from all pain. In fact, the Lord instructs us to deal with all melancholy: "...Remove sorrow from your heart." (Ecclesiastes 11:10). The only way I know how to remove sorrow is by pouring out my sadness before God in prayer. It is amazing how close you feel to your Heavenly Father as you share it all with Him. You will not only get healed but you will also get closer to God at the same time.

We all go through difficulties and disappointments and get hurt along the way. People let us down, making it hard for us to trust. Our dreams may get dashed, leaving us heavy-hearted. Things can happen that make us sad. But because we love the Lord, we normally just dust ourselves down and carry on. We bury the pain and move on. Most of us treat our cars better than our hearts. We take our vehicle for a regular service but how often do we take time out to repair the wear and tear in our soul? What do you do with disappointments and how do you deal with life's let-downs? That is why I believe God created our ministry Healed for Life. It is like a spiritual service for the soul, to deal with every hidden hurt that is hindering our lives. We leave feeling light, refreshed and free. Tamar never dealt with the traumas and trials of her life and she remained desolate. If you want to be free to fulfill your

God-given destiny, I encourage you to make a prayerful decision today to embrace a life of healing.

Let's Change Our Ways

In the next chapter, we are going to look at the extraordinary example of King David. He is the biblical antidote to internalization. I believe you will learn a new way of living your life. It takes practice at first, but the joy and freedom that follow are phenomenal. For now, though, let's deal with the issue of internalization in prayer. It is not God's way, so we need to ask Him for His help to change. Let's pray.

Heavenly Father,

You are such a kind, good God. I am so grateful that You want me to be free from all stress and sadness. I realize that I often ignore my emotions and push down my pain. There have been times when it has been too uncomfortable to acknowledge my emotions. On other occasions, I didn't even know what was going on inside. I might have habitually pushed down pain and ignored my feelings. I may have belittled their importance. I am sorry for every time that I have internalized. I now realize that it is unhealthy. Forgive me, Lord. You designed me to feel and express the full range of emotions. You want me to share my heart with You through every up and down in life. Please help me to release my inner issues and to express myself in Your presence. Change me, I pray, and lead me into a lifelong journey of intimacy with You.

In Jesus' name, I pray,

Amen.

Chapter 6
THE DAVID WAY

When the Lord looked over the life of King David from the vantage point of the New Testament, He gave the royal psalmist a resounding endorsement. Acts 13:22 records God's assessment of him: 'I have found David the son of Jesse, a man after My own heart, who will do all My will.' What an extraordinary statement. The Lord described David as a man after His own heart. I would suggest that we therefore see the shepherd king as a role model. The good thing is that God has given us a window into this leader's heart. That's because David revealed his desires, aversions and thoughts in the psalms, half of which were written by him.

Reading Psalms...

I am going to be very honest. I always enjoyed reading the uplifting passages in the Psalms. I would dwell on the faith-building and inspirational verses and knew many by heart. I would often quote "Bless the Lord O my soul and forget not all of His benefits..." (Psalm 103:1). I would eagerly read "One thing I have desired of the Lord, that will I seek: that I may dwell in the house of the Lord all the days of my life..." (Psalms 27:4). By contrast, when I reached the negative verses, I would jump past them until I found more positivity. I had enough of my own issues without drowning in David's problems! I know I'm not alone! If you're a regular Bible reader, you have probably done that too.

The Real Deal

So why is all that struggle and sadness written in scripture? Nothing in the Bible is there by accident. It is written for a purpose. I am convinced that the psalms provide us with a guide to a healthy heart life. Although some psalms are songs, many are reflections or prayers. In my view, the 75 chapters penned by the king are more of a journal than a hymn book. David treated the Lord like his closest confidante. He told God about every stress and strain. He shared his happiest highs, but he also talked to the Lord about his heartbreaking lows. David bared his soul before his Father in Heaven.

Psalm 13 is written by the man that God said had a heart after His own. Let's read it in the Message: "Long enough, God - you've ignored me long enough. I've looked at the back of your head long enough. Long enough I've carried this ton of trouble, lived with a stomach full of pain. Long enough my arrogant enemies have looked down their noses at me." Let us reflect for a moment. David vented his frustration in God's presence. The king was not afraid to tell the Lord that he felt ignored. David told God that he was bewildered and confused. Most believers are unable to tell their Heavenly Father how they really feel for fear of offending Him. So, we either suppress the feeling or tell someone else instead. Neither option helps. God knows what you think anyway. When you tell Him the truth, it deepens your relationship. Not only that, when you release your frustrations in prayer, you will leave your secret place feeling relieved. He desires truth in the inward parts so that our hearts can be made whole.

The Turn Around

The passage continues: "Take a good look at me, God, my God; I want to look life in the eye, so no enemy can get the best of me or laugh when I fall on my face." David's attitude was turning. He was no longer bewildered (because he poured it out) and the will to fight arose again within him. The king stopped blaming the Lord and instead began seeking the Holy Spirit's help. David started holding his real enemies to account. Let us now read the final few verses of Psalm 13 in the Message: "I've thrown myself headlong into your arms - I'm celebrating your rescue. I'm singing at the top of my lungs, I'm so full of answered prayers." What a turnaround! David went from bleak bewilderment to overflowing thankfulness in one prayer session. You see, when we release our issues in the presence of God, we are free to get back on track.

Feeling Forgotten

Have you ever felt forgotten? It is one thing to think that people have abandoned you. It is quite another to feel jilted by God. The truth is, I think that we have all felt like that at some time or another. Dreams may fade to a flickering memory because decades have passed while we waited. One disappointment after another may start to make you feel like one big disappointment. It is all too easy to feel forsaken by the One who promised us a better life.

David clearly felt that the Lord had let him down. King Saul, the man that David once called father, hated the shepherd boy with such passion that he commissioned armies to murder him. The young man had been promised that he would be king. However, all he encountered on every side was unbelievable hardship and bitter hatred. He did not live in a palace. He lived rough. He was always on the move, fearing daily for his life. He had no royal robes. Instead, he probably watched the clothes on his back wear out day by day. When David went into prayer, he was deeply disheartened.

The God's Honest Truth

Perhaps you are trying your hardest to provide for your family. You are desperate to create a better life for the ones you love. However, no matter how hard you work, you seem to fall flat on your face. You struggle to pay the bills, you are not living in the home you had hoped for and you cannot take the family on those special vacations. When you were younger, you believed that you would have been somewhere by now. You thought that you would have accomplished something significant by this time. Instead, when you look around, all you feel is shame. Maybe you watch others making progress, doing well and leading fulfilling lives. But when you look in the mirror, you see a shadow of the person that you had hoped you would become.

It might not be an all-consuming issue for you, but you feel a sense of embarrassment about your lot in life. You may not even have acknowledged it before because staring that kind of truth in the face can be intensely uncomfortable. David knew what it was to feel that way. In Psalm 22:6-7, the psalmist told God: "I am a worm, and no man; a reproach of men, and despised by the people. All those who see me ridicule me; they shoot out the lip, they shake the head...". He was saying: "God I feel like a complete nobody. I am the one that others step on and walk all over. I feel humiliated and squashed. Everybody thinks I'm a complete joke, and the truth is, so do I." Every time David poured out his pain in prayer, he left God's presence strengthened and encouraged.

Up and Down!

When we read the psalms, we may assume that David was an emotional yo-yo! From one verse to the next, he contradicts himself. Yet that shows the power of his prayers. He told God how he felt and then commanded his heart to believe the truth. He shared his deepest issues with the Lover of his soul and then told his heart to have faith. In Psalm 42:9, David said how he felt: "Why have You forgotten me?" Then a few moments later in verse 11, he encouraged himself: "Why are you cast down, O my soul? And why are you disquieted within me? Hope in God..."

I have done this many times. Just recently, I was feeling heavy. I was overtired and discouraged. At the start of my prayer time I told the Lord how low I felt. I shared my heart with my Heavenly Father. Afterwards, I reminded myself of God's goodness and His promises to me. When we are real with God, we can release any sadness or negativity, leaving our hearts free to believe again.

Low Point

Psalm 22 is famous because it is a prophecy about the anguish that Jesus went through on the cross. However, when David was writing, I don't believe he knew he was prophesying. Psalm 22 is also an account of a young man crying out to God about the agony he was enduring. Bible historians tell us that this psalm was written at Ziklag - the place where David lost his family, his possessions and his city. To make matters even worse, in the midst of his agony, his leaders turned on him and wanted to take his life. David felt completely forgotten and expressed his deep disappointment with God: "My God, my God, why have you abandoned me? Why are you so far away when I groan for help?" (Psalm 22:1 NLT).

David poured out his pain. Then, when his grief had been released, he was able to strengthen himself again and ask the Spirit of God for direction. It is very hard to hear God when we are angry and hurt. However, when we pour out our hearts in prayer and release our anguish, we are able to listen to the Lord again. After David prayed, his peace returned. God then gave him instructions that led to the greatest turnaround of his life. David found his family, recovered his people's possessions and, within a week, was crowned king. I do not believe that David would have been capable of leading his men to victory that day if he had not first dealt with his anguish. After his heart was healed, he could hear heaven's strategy and lay hold of the strength he needed to achieve resounding success. When are hearts are free from clutter, we can be both sensitive and strong.

He Can Handle It!

I do not think that God gets worried when we tell Him how we are feeling. In Psalm 44:23, the sons of Korah were weary and weighed down. They were fed up of fighting and cried out to God: "Awake! Why do You sleep O Lord?"

Let me ask you a question: does God ever sleep? No, that's right. The Bible makes it clear that He never slumbers or sleeps in Psalm 121:4. So why is Psalm 44 in the Bible? I believe that many verses in the Psalms are there for you and I to learn that it is okay to be real in prayer. God wants us to express our inner angst to Him. It creates intimacy. Once we have released our frustration, then we can return to the truth and get ourselves back on track. This is how David lived life. When something terrible happened, the king would rush into the presence of the Lord to pour out his pain. He would tell God what had happened and how it hurt. He spoke to the Lord like a child to his father. We were made to express ourselves. Matthew 12:34 says: "Out of the overflow of the heart, the mouth speaks." God made us this way for a purpose. Our mouths are the release mechanism for our inner man. Just as a pressure cooker needs a release valve, so our souls must have an outlet for all the energy that emotions produce.

Precious To God

Psalms 56:8 says, "You keep track of all my sorrows. You have collected all my tears in your bottle. You have recorded each one in your book." Why would the Lord keep our tears in a bottle? Why would He take notes every time we cry before Him? This verse tells us that the tears we pour out in His presence are very precious to Him. Has anyone ever shared their heart with you when you were not expecting it? Maybe it was someone you respected or a person that you did not know so well. It can feel like a tremendous privilege when someone trusts us enough to open up and share their lives with us. In the same way, God treasures every moment that you share your heart with Him. He values you more than you could know. So when you choose to pour out your pain in prayer, He takes notes. He listens lovingly and attentively. I believe He holds your tears as mementoes of your time together.

Who Is God To You?

Let us look at Psalm 23. David was a shepherd and he risked everything to protect his sheep. Rather than losing one little lamb, David fought off both a lion and a bear. He stayed with his flock on the top of the mountain, day and night, through sun and snow. When David declared: "The Lord is my shepherd", he was exclaiming: "God is my helper, my protector, my guardian, my source. He will never let me down. He will never leave me and He will risk everything to make sure I am well." Our God has more names than anyone else I know. He has a name for every need you have. He is the answer to every issue you are facing. Not only does He want to give you a way out, He wants to be your way out.

Jesus instructed us in the gospels to come to Him as little children. When a child falls over, they will run into their mother's arms and tell her exactly what happened and where they are hurting. They will cry while their mom cuddles them. Soon enough they are well again.

In contrast, when you and I talk to God, more often than not we approach Him as grown-ups. We don't share the things that are troubling our hearts. We tell Him what we think He wants to hear. Imagine that you have a humiliating meeting at work that leaves you stripped of your self-respect. Your first response might be anger. You probably suppress the feeling and try your best to get on with your day. When you get home, you may be so agitated that you slam some doors or snap at the kids. When you next pray, if you even tell the Lord about your day, you may say something like this: "God, deal with my boss!"

Shame is excruciating and humiliation hurts. If we pray the David way, we would be more likely to say something like this: "Lord, I felt completely stripped of my dignity today. My co-workers humiliated me with their jokes and jibes. I felt stupid and it hurt. Please heal my heart, Lord." When we tell God how we are really feeling, we can leave our secret place free. David poured his hurts out and ended up encouraged. We push them down and end up discouraged. The more we release distress in prayer, the more we will experience joy in life.

David Paved The Way

David expressed a wide range of emotions in the psalms. He was angry in Psalm 35 and eager to see his enemies brought to justice. He asked God to send angels to chase them. He hoped they would die! David was dealing with deep discouragement in Psalm 12. He was fed up with the hypocrisy of the people around him and wondered if anyone righteous was left. In Psalm 3, he was confused. Despite persistent prayer, his problems got worse.

Whatever the trial, the king expressed and released his frustration and pain in the presence of God. He came into his prayer closet heavy laden but left with a lightness in his spirit. David was heartbroken in Psalm 6:6. He said, "I am weary with my groaning; all night I make my bed swim; I drench my couch with tears." He cried all night long in the arms of his Heavenly Father. He didn't suppress his sadness. He poured it out in prayer. By morning, he began to feel lighter. Hope arose on the inside and he responded, "The Lord has heard the voice of my weeping. The Lord has heard my supplication." Psalm 6:8-9.

When we feel guilty, we often try to forget what we have done. Discomfort builds on the inside and we try to distance ourselves from our mistakes. Sadly, sometimes we avoid the Lord. Not David. In Psalm 38, he came to God and gave Him his guilt. There are two extremely unpleasant emotions that David frequently faced. The first was betrayal and the second was rejection. Let us look at how he dealt with these soul-destroying experiences.

Broken Trust and its Consequences

Trust is the glue that holds relationships together. When trust is broken, it can be devastating. The very people we believed we could rely upon let us down. It creates a distressing mixture of disbelief and disappointment. David suffered many heartbreaking betrayals by friends, family and staff. His son tried to steal the throne from under his feet. One of his leaders persuaded the people to desert David. His friend forsook him when the king needed his help the most.

God is able to work all things together for our good (Romans 8:28). At the same time, satan is seeking to twist our worst circumstances around for greater evil. He wants to turn every trial into a tragedy and every betrayal into a full-blown bust up. The devil wants to use betrayal to stop you trusting and believing. We can forgive those who betray us, but unless our hearts are healed, we will struggle to trust again. If a church leader lets you down, the temptation may be to doubt the integrity of all ministers. If a teacher hurts your child, you may end up being suspicious of all educators. If a former boyfriend breaks your heart, you may become wary of all men. If a previous prayer partner spreads your secrets, you may keep all church folk at arm's length. That is a problem because trust is the atmosphere for faith. God uses people to help us fulfill our purpose. If we cannot trust people, we may miss our destiny.

What Did David Do?

You guessed it. He did not spill his soul to his friends. He did not withdraw from fellowship. He told God exactly what happened: "They visit me as if they were my friends, but all the while they gather gossip, and when they leave, they spread it everywhere. All who hate me whisper about me, imagining the worst." Psalms 41:6-7 (NLT). David articulated the agony: "All day long they twist my words. All their thoughts are against me for evil..." Psalm 56:5.

Have you been lied about? Have people you trusted taken your words and twisted them? Or have you been accused of things you didn't do? It hurts terribly. However, the Lord is able to heal your heart. Betrayal creates a sense of disbelief. We cannot fathom what they have done. That one who we would have trusted with our life turns around and backstabs. This disbelief and shock must be expressed for it to be relieved. You need to say the words that you feel, but you need to express them to the right person. When we continuously tell the people around us what happened, we end up seething and hurting all the more. However, when we share every sense of incredulity with the Lord, He can actually do something about it. He can bring relief.

Give It To God

Each time he was wounded, Israel's greatest king went straight to his Heavenly Father to be healed. In Psalm 55, David described the devastation to God in detail: "It is not an enemy who reproaches me; then I could bear it. Nor is it one who hates me who has exalted himself against me; then I could hide from him. But it was you, a man my equal, my companion and my acquaintance." (Psalms 55:12-13). David's emotional issues were dealt with in the presence of God. He went through hell and was healed of his turmoil and tragedy.

You may be reading this and thinking trusting again is total foolishness. Why would I want to believe in people after I have been betrayed? As the expression goes, 'Once bitten, twice shy'. Let me explain... Like you, I have been betrayed many times. People I trusted have broken my heart. However, it never stopped there. Each time, I did what I'm encouraging you to do. I did it so often it became a lifestyle. God healed me in the depths of my inner being countless times. He took all my pain away so that all that remained inside for the 'perpetrators' was sincere love. In short, I can trust people because I trust God. I know that the Lord is well able to take care of my heart. If I get betrayed again, He will heal me again. In the meantime, I enjoy life.

The Caveat

Although David was restored in many amazing ways, I don't think he was ever completely healed. Deep-rooted parental rejection affected him his whole life. Despite multiple mentions of his father, siblings, aunts, uncles and even grandparents, we hear nothing about David's mother. I suspect the "conceived in sin" reference in Psalm 139 meant exactly that. Jesse had sons with his wife, but perhaps he fathered David with another woman. Maybe David was the fruit of an affair. In Psalm 27:10, David cried out to God about his deep sense of rejection: "... My father and my mother have forsaken me..." (Amplified). He was saying, "My mom and my dad didn't want me."

David felt forsaken by both his father and his mother. Although he learned how to pour out his heart before the Lord, I don't believe he experienced the kind of structural healing that could have saved his family. I have no doubt that David derived his value from the Lord. He experienced a good measure of healing in the depths of his heart. However, the work was not complete. How do I know? Well, it is in our most intimate relationships that we discover how healed we really are. Moses gave clear instructions in Deuteronomy 17:17 on how kings of Israel should behave: "Neither shall he multiply wives for himself, lest his heart turn away..." Yet David seemed to pick up a new woman in every city. He seemed to crave their love.

It Always Shows

It continues... David was not a great dad. He did not know how to handle his sons when they went astray. As we learned in the last chapter, three of his children - Amnon, Absalom and Tamar - got into a tragic mess. Amnon raped Tamar and David did not deal with his son's abominable abuse. As a result, Absalom took matters into his own hands and killed Amnon for defiling their sister. David did not learn from his mistakes. After the murder, David did not handle Absalom the right way either. Consequently, the young man's heart was poisoned and his life was cut short. Pouring out our pain is vital to our well-being. David proves that it is crucial but the journey does not stop there. Once we have poured out our pain, we need to be filled with His supernatural love and fully restored. The next two chapters will help you understand how to receive transformational healing. First, let us recap what we have learned from one of the Bible's greatest leaders.

Learning From The Leader

King David voiced the agonizing and uncomfortable issues buried in his heart. He did not detach himself from pain or shame. He did not deny the truth because it was too hard to face. He did not turn away because it was easier to ignore his inner issues. He did what most of us have never done. He got into the presence of God and told the Lord exactly how he felt. He told his dearest friend about the deepest needs of his heart. He was true and he was real: "I called on the Lord in my distress, the Lord answered me and set me in a broad place..." (Psalm 118:5)

Psalm 62:8 declares, "Pour out your heart before Him." This is not an invitation. It is an instruction. Some of the directions God gives us are for our physical fitness. Many are for our spiritual well-being. This is for our emotional health and it is vital. Psalm 84:5 says: "Blessed is the man whose strength is in You. Whose heart is set on pilgrimage, as they pass through the valley of baca, they make it a spring..." Baca means weeping. The tears you release in prayer will turn your river of pain into a spring of healing to refresh many. My Emotional Manual at the back of this book will help you deal with a whole range of difficult feelings. Let us pray.

Heavenly Father,

Thank You for the wonderful example of David's prayer life. He was a mighty leader who was tender in Your presence. I ask You to help me to articulate my deepest issues in prayer. Teach me how to bring every sadness and disappointment straight to You. Help me to express my anger and frustration before You. I want to be completely real with You. Please forgive me for the times when I have been quick to share with others but slow to open up with You. You are my Father and my closest friend. From today I ask You to teach me how to pray the David way. I want to learn how to talk to You the way You desire. I love You with all of my heart.

In Jesus' name I pray,

Amen.

Chapter 7
LOVE WITH STRINGS ATTACHED

When we know that our parents loved us while we were growing up, we sometimes assume that we should be immune to problems in later life. Although my family went through more than its fair share of trauma, I always believed that I was loved. My inner turmoil therefore made no sense to me. As a result, I asked the Lord to show me why I was so full of insecurities in my early adult life. The Holy Spirit whispered two words: "Conditional love." I had never heard the phrase before and yet I immediately understood. Those words shed light on a deep-rooted source of rejection felt by a huge majority of people.

Conditional love is love with strings attached. When I use that phrase, you may think of a young man putting pressure on a young woman to have sex before marriage. However, that is not what I am talking about. Conditional love frequently has its origins in how we were raised. Perhaps you were only really affirmed when you achieved. Maybe you were celebrated only when you succeeded. It could be that you were treated kindly only when you were sick. Did you ever feel that you had to earn the approval of your parents?

The Impact

When we believe that the love of our parents is dependent upon our behavior, it can make us feel inadequate and insecure. We feel inadequate because we believe that we are not enough without our efforts or achievements. We feel insecure because we assume that the love of our carers could be withdrawn at any moment. Rejection sets in because we think that "the real me" is not wanted. Living with such insecurity is tiring. No matter how many times we are celebrated, it is never enough. There is a constant need for affirmation and approval. We never feel like we are sufficient.

Before we go any further, I would like to highlight something important. I have never seen a baby born with an instruction manual strapped to its thigh! When you arrived, your parents probably did their best with what they had. Hurt people inevitably hurt people so if your father or mother was wounded, he or she will probably have caused you some pain along the way. To face our imperfect upbringings is not to criticize our families. It is simply part of the process of our restoration. It is imperative that you acknowledge the ways that your upbringing affected both your view of yourself and the state of your soul.

Affection And Affirmation

God's original plan was that every single one of us would grow up knowing the unconditional love of both our father and our mother. Just as a plant needs the sunshine to survive, so we need the warmth and affection of our parents to thrive. Constant cuddles tell a child that they are precious. Punctuating the day with kind smiles communicates acceptance. A regular reassuring arm around your shoulder creates security. Without any words, it relays the message, "You're special."

It is not just kindness that is important. In the same way that a trellis or a bamboo cane provides the structure and support for a plant to grow tall, so our parents' words of belief and affirmation enable us to grow and excel. Proverbs 4:3 expresses how our parents should make us feel: "When I was my father's son, tender and the only one in the sight of my mother." A father's affection should be tender and a mother's love should make us feel like we are the only one in the world. When a plant is not nurtured in the right conditions, its growth is stunted. If you did not receive unchanging parental love expressed with both warmth and words, it will probably have affected your soul. We can never overestimate the impact that our upbringing has on our inner wellbeing. There is healing. Your heart can be made whole, your soul restored and your life greatly enhanced.

Cut To The Heart

King Saul struggled with insecurities throughout his reign. He felt inadequate when God called him. He felt threatened when folk celebrated David and he hankered after the approval and praises of the people. Hurt people inevitably hurt people and King Saul is no exception. I am sure that the king loved his son but his affection fluctuated. He lashed out at his son, hurling hurtful words at his own flesh and blood: "Saul boiled with rage at Jonathan. 'You stupid son of a whore!' he swore at him..." (1 Samuel 20:30 NLT). Coming from his father, these ruthless remarks must have lacerated Jonathan's heart. Proverbs 12:18 says, "There is one who speaks like the piercing of a sword." When cruel comments come from a parent, they hurt all the more. It did not stop there. "Then Saul hurled his spear at Jonathan, intending to kill him." 1 Samuel 20:33 (NLT). Maybe Jonathan always knew that his dad loved him. However, Saul's love was far from unconditional.

Is This Your Story?

Although no two childhood experiences are the same, we may have dealt with similar problems. As you read the paragraphs that follow, you may find that one scenario sums up your experiences or there may be threads of your story running through them all. Allow the the Spirit of God to help you recognize what was missing in your upbringing. When we know what hurt us, we can face the pain and be healed.

Driven

When you were growing up, were words of praise almost exclusively associated with success? When you excelled at school or sport, were you celebrated? When you didn't, were you merely tolerated? Did you grow up believing that when you behaved well, you would be loved? Maybe you strived to secure praise by becoming a high achiever.

Distant

Perhaps your dad was distant. He could have left when you were young or maybe he stayed but he never felt close. He got up and went to work, then he came home and went to bed. Was he strict and scary, only really talking to you about school or homework? Maybe you didn't spend any special time together. Possibly you don't remember much affection or kindness. He may have provided for you or even given you gifts, but he was never emotionally involved in your life. This might be a description of your mother, or even both your parents. Perhaps you were adopted or fostered and you never knew your biological mum and dad.

Punishing

When you were naughty, did you feel like love was withdrawn? Perhaps when you were punished, your parents sent you out of their presence. Maybe when you failed they treated you with scorn. Were you left alone to cry for hours? Did a parent's attitude towards you change - as though your mistake made you a mistake? Undue harshness can be devastating. Colossians 3:21 in the Amplified says, "Fathers, do not provoke or irritate or fret your children [do not be hard on them or harass them], lest they become discouraged and sullen and morose and feel inferior and frustrated. [Do not break their spirit.]" Punishment without love can cause us to break inside.

Think back to the way you felt when you were corrected. Was it simply sadness that you missed the mark? Or did you, in fact, feel rejected? Proverbs 3:12 says, "For whom the Lord loves He corrects, just as a father the son in whom he delights." Although correction can be painful, the Lord's plan is that it is an expression of parental love. If you were on the receiving end of unloving admonition, it may have left a deep mark.

No Rules

Maybe you grew up without boundaries. You were left to make up your own mind about bedtime and behavior. You could watch what you wanted and hang out with anyone you fancied. Sounds great, doesn't it? In reality, it damages our view of our value. Anything precious comes with clear instructions. Proverbs 22:6 makes it clear that parents are supposed to instruct their children: "Train up a child in the way he should go, and when he is old he will not depart from it." The absence of boundaries can communicate a lack of concern. It can make us believe that we are not important enough to warrant any parental worry.

Control & Criticism

Did you have a controlling or critical mother or carer? Perhaps every decision you made was queried or criticized. You were told that your outfit didn't match or that your friends dressed better than you. Your school work was scrutinized and your best efforts were never good enough. You were told what to wear and what to say on every important occasion. Control can crush our confidence and constant criticism can tear us down. You may have felt that you weren't capable of anything. Perhaps you were afraid to make a mistake. 1 Corinthians 13:7 in the Amplified explains: Love... is ever ready to believe the best of every person..." Control, by definition, does not believe or trust. It doubts, imposes and can be very destructive.

If you experienced this sort of upbringing, you may have become a perfectionist in adult life. Perhaps you constantly seek to attain impossibly high standards. On the other hand, you may doubt your own decision-making and shun responsibility. These issues might leave very deep roots.

Abject Abandonment or Brutal Abuse

Perhaps your upbringing was cruel, cold and frightening. There was no tenderness or kindness. You somehow survived, but your life was shattered. You may have been saved for some years and learned something of the goodness of God. I believe He wants to go to the roots of your rejection and create in you an understanding of His love and your value.

All of these experiences create a deep sense of instability. If I believe that my behavior can change a parent's perspective of me, that will probably make me feel unsafe. If love comes with strings attached, then it makes us feel as though we have to work for approval. Conditional love makes us feel as though we need to earn the right to be loved. Deep down inside we end up believing statements such as: "I'm only valuable if I'm achieving" or "I'm only lovable if I'm behaving".

What is Unconditional Love?

Several years ago, my son came home from school with an appalling report. Teachers commented that his behavior was poor, he was distracting others and he was not putting in any effort. His homework was half-hearted and his organizational skills were distinctly lacking. God had made the way for our children to get free places at one of the best schools in Britain so it seemed like he was squandering a sensational opportunity. I was very disappointed. I sat down with him and told him that this was completely unacceptable. This was the strongest discussion I had ever had with my son. I told him how he would be punished. No computer games or socializing for one month. I was tough!

As our ten minute discussion drew to a close, I began to feel uneasy. So before I told him he could go, I enquired, "You do know that daddy and I love you, don't you? We are extremely unhappy with your attitude and behavior, but you do know that we still love you?" His response came without hesitation. With a calm smile, he replied, "Of course I do, mummy." Then he left the room. I sat amazed at the goodness of God. Benjy was well aware that he had seriously missed the mark. He knew everything about his approach to school had to change. He was ashamed of his behavior and upset that he would have to go a whole month without his favorite games. However, he did not feel rejected even for a moment. He knew that he was utterly loved, irrespective of his flaws or failings.

Unconditional love is not a phrase that appears in Scripture. Having said that, God's unconditional love for His people is demonstrated from the beginning to the end of the Bible. It means loving someone just as they are, no matter what they do or fail to do. When a child knows that they are loved unconditionally, they will feel secure in the knowledge that neither their actions nor their inactions could lessen the love that they enjoy.

The Greatest

The greatest description of true love is found in 1 Corinthians 13:4-7. Let's look at verses 4 and 7 in the Amplified Bible: "Love endures long and is patient and kind... Love bears up under anything and everything that comes, is ever ready to believe the best of every person, its hopes are fadeless under all circumstances, and it endures everything [without weakening]." Ideally, we would be able to replace the word love with 'mum' or 'dad' and make ourselves the recipients of such powerful emotion. That is unconditional love.

This kind of love is not shaken and it does not come and go. It is complete and consistent. It cannot be earned, it is a given and it is dependable. We see the unconditional love of God displayed towards Israel throughout the Old Testament. He creates boundaries, disciplines His children when they go astray, pursues them even when they turn their backs on Him and welcomes each one with open arms when they return. His love does not fluctuate based on behavior. He rewards obedience and deals with sinfulness, but His love for His people never changes.

Facing The Truth

In the light of the descriptions we have just read and with reference to the picture of true love, it's time to ask yourself if you have any wounds resulting from conditional love. I think love with strings attached is one of the least understood and yet most common causes of insecurity in men and women across the world.

God wants to do a wonderful work in the depths of your innermost being. I don't know your story but I do know that there is nothing that He can't mend. The Holy Spirit wants to shine His light onto those hidden hurts and bring healing. He unearths buried, even forgotten, sadness so that He can bring restoration in the recesses of our souls.

It is time to face your pain. Maybe it was what was said and done to you: cruel words, harsh discipline, outbursts of rage, constant criticism, put-downs or continual comparisons with siblings and friends. You may even have suffered abuse or neglect. Maybe it is what you didn't receive. Perhaps you never knew what it was like to have your father put his reassuring arm around your shoulder. Maybe you never heard your mum tell you that she loved you just because you were her princess. Perhaps your parents didn't tell you that they were proud of you just the way you were. Maybe you never felt like they were overjoyed to have you in their lives. On the other hand, maybe you never knew your mum or dad and you have faced a lifelong vacuum where security and identity should have been. God wants to heal your heart.

Right now, I encourage you to pour out your heart and pray this prayer:

Heavenly Father,

I now realize that I grew up believing that love was conditional. I felt that the affection of those who cared for me might come and go depending upon my actions. It made me feel insecure and unsure of myself. Even now, I feel as though I am constantly having to work to earn the love of the people around me.

I remember when (now tell the Lord about any memories that the Holy Spirit has brought to your mind. Tell the Lord what happened in as much detail as you can and how all that made you feel. Pour out your heart like water before the Lord). It hurts. I give you my pain. Please take it away, I pray. It is too much for me. I have been striving for much of my life and I have had enough. Heal my heart, oh Lord.

In Jesus' name, I pray,

Amen.

Filling The Vacuum

Once we have had our pain taken away, we need to receive a revelation of the Lord's unchanging love. You might say that you know God loves you. This is different. When we really understand that we are completely and perfectly loved just the way we are, all striving for acceptance ceases. It is like pouring concrete into the foundations of a building. It creates great stability and security, which in turn produce a peace that makes you completely comfortable in your own skin. Before we continue, let's pause for a moment and ask the Lord to open our eyes and our hearts to the enormity of His love.

Heavenly Father,

I pray that You will help me to understand the depth of Your love for me. Help me to grasp how much You love me, just as I am. Before You formed me, You already knew me and delighted in me. Help me to realize that You love me perfectly and completely. Open my eyes to understand Your Word in my heart and to receive the truth that it brings.

In Jesus' name, I pray,

Amen.

Let's look at what the Bible teaches us about the quality and enormity of God's love for you.

Always Loved

"But God shows and clearly proves His [own] love for us by the fact that while we were still sinners, Christ (the Messiah, the Anointed One) died for us." (Romans 5:8 Amplified). I want you to imagine yourself at your lowest point. For some of you that might be a long time ago. For others that might be right now. I want you to picture that version of yourself. The God of heaven and earth loved and loves you with all His heart - then and now. He was not - and will never be - put off by any of our ugliness. His love searched you out at your lowest point. He gave everything in life and in death just so that He could win you over and have you by His side.

First Loved

"We love Him because He first loved us." (1 John 4:19). God does not love you because you love Him. He does not love you because you are thoughtful or faithful. His affection is not based upon the purity of your faith. He loved you before you even knew what love was. He loves you because you are His. He loved you first.

Completely Loved

"See what [an incredible] quality of love the Father has given (shown, bestowed on) us, that we should [be permitted to] be named and called and counted the children of God! And so we are! ..." (1 John 3:1 Amplified). Sometimes we believe that if we pray longer or read the Bible more, then we might be able to earn just a little bit more of the Lord's love.

A few years ago, I was listening to a teaching by Joyce Meyer. She made the point that God would never love me more than He loved me at that moment because He already loved me with all His heart. These words pierced my heart and I started to cry. These were not tears of joy. I was sad that I could not do anything to get God to love me just a little bit more. For years, I had subconsciously been working to earn His affections. The truth dawned on me. I clearly had no real understanding of how much He already loved me.

Self-image is the picture I have of myself. It is what I think of me. It will determine my thoughts, attitudes and behavior. It will influence who I become. So it is important that my view of myself is a healthy one. For many years, I had no problem loving myself. After all, God loves me. However, I struggled to like myself. I thought I was efficient, focused and well organized, but not really very likeable. If you had asked me if my husband or close friends liked me, I would have said, "Of course!" However, if you had asked me if they were *right* to like me, I would have faltered. What do you think of yourself? You may be very sure of your strengths and confident in your gifts, but do you like *you*? Would you choose yourself as a friend? Self-image is forged at a young age and, whether you acknowledge it or not, your view of yourself shapes your life.

The Power Of Love

Jane was one of my childhood friends. She was raised in a distinctly dysfunctional family. She had a host of stepsisters, lived with a spiteful stepmother and endured years of separation from both her biological parents. She had every reason to have a damaged self-image. However, in all the years that I knew Jane, she always liked herself. This puzzled me. I knew people from "normal" families who didn't really like themselves. Yet this woman from a broken home had a great self-image. I asked God why and what He showed me was amazing.

Jane always knew that both her father and her mother loved her unconditionally. Despite the mess that occurred, they constantly told her of their unchanging love. Her mother would write her letters that described in great detail how much she adored her daughter. Throughout her childhood, Jane's father would sit her on his lap, wrap his arms around her and tell her how delighted he was that she was his little girl. Jane understood the unconditional love of God because she had been cherished throughout her childhood by both her parents. As a result, Jane liked herself.

When you know that you are perfectly loved, you will like yourself, despite your imperfections. When you don't really like yourself, it is usually because you have not yet understood the unreserved love that your Heavenly Father has for you. As I began to understand that nothing I did or said would (or even could) change God's love for me, I began to unravel on the inside. The realization that I was unconditionally loved stabilized me. Soon, I started to not only love myself, but to like myself too.

Insecurity, instability, poor self-image, defensiveness and low self-worth all point to the fact that we don't know that we are unconditionally loved by the Lord of heaven and earth. They are all evidence that you need to understand, perhaps for the first time, that you are completely and perfectly loved by the greatest father the world has ever known.

His Love Makes You Whole

"I pray that... your roots will grow down into God's love and... that you understand... how wide, how long, how high, and how deep His love is. May you experience the love of Christ, though it is too great to understand fully. Then you will be made complete..." Ephesians 3:16-19 (New Living Translation). Let's start by looking at the end of this verse. It says, "*Then* you will be made complete..." Complete means whole, lacking nothing. God's desire is that your heart is whole. He wants you to have the deepest sense of security. He longs to give you certainty that you are enough and the reassurance that you are sufficient just the way you are because you belong to Him. What will make this a reality in your soul? There are two important parts of the process.

1. Receiving your healing is the starting point. We need to allow the Lord to take us on a journey. By grace, He has already started a work in you. However, I have never seen God bring complete healing to a person's heart in one encounter with His healing love. The inner thoughts and heart of man are deep (Psalm 64:6), so the process of restoration takes time. We need to allow God to minister to each corner and crevice of our hearts. Each occasion that we encounter His healing, we get closer to Jesus and get to know Him more intimately. The very process is precious because it draws us deeper into our relationship with the Lord. We get restored, but also rejuvenated deep down.

2. As well as being healed, you need to receive a revelation of the magnitude of God's unchanging love for you. Your Heavenly Father wants you to know and believe in the depths of your being that you are utterly and perfectly loved. The Lord wants you to realize that He loves you with all of His heart and that there is nothing you could do to make Him love you any less or any more. You already have all His love. You are cherished.

When you are truly healed of all your hurts and you also understand the Lord's unchanging love, you will become secure and stable. You will know an amazing sense of peace. I would love to lead you in prayer, that you will receive a life-changing revelation and infilling of His love right now - like never before.

Heavenly Father,

I have read about Your love, but now I want to experience it. I am sorry for every lie I have believed that I could earn Your love. I ask You to forgive me for every wrong belief that I have had about Your love. Now I know that You love me completely, You love me just because I am your child. You love me when I am doing the right thing and when I am in the wrong. Help me to understand the vast width, length, height and depth of Your love for me. I receive Your love right now. I believe Your supernatural love. Fill me to overflowing with Your wonderful, unchanging love. I know now that You love me completely and You love me perfectly and I thank You with all my heart. I receive Your love.

In the name of Jesus, I pray,

Amen.

Chapter 8
REMOVAL OF APPROVAL

Have you ever felt that awful churning in the pit of your stomach? Have you experienced that unease that arises on the inside when you fear you have upset someone significant? Maybe you made a mistake or forgot an appointment. Perhaps you said something wrong or stepped out of line. You think that you did something to antagonize or disappoint that all-important person. Their approval has lifted and in its place, you assume that a cloak of disapproval has descended. You have a sinking feeling, an intense disquiet. You feel that the only way to alleviate the distress is to recover that person's approval and to enjoy the sunshine of their pleasure once again.

Preoccupation with the opinions of other people is a major issue which affects a large number of Christians. I encourage you to read my book Dreamstealers. It looks at seven heart diseases that try to steal destinies. The fear of man - which I cover in detail - is one of the most dangerous. As you read, the Holy Spirit will show you the road to freedom. Here, we are going to look at a very specific and subtle form of the fear of man that seeks to creep into all our lives.

Proverbs 29:26 in the Amplified says, "Many crave and seek the ruler's favor, but the wise man [waits] for justice from the Lord." The ruler in this scenario is the dominant figure in your life whose opinion means the most. Often we long for validation from that one person. When we have their endorsement, all is well. You might say that you no longer crave affirmation. However, how do you feel if that all-important person is displeased?

I had been delivered from the general fear of man and reached a place where my heart was set on pleasing God, not people. I could handle being rejected and no longer longed to be liked. I thought I was free. Then the Holy Spirit shone His light into my heart and revealed a pattern in my reactions...

There were three people whose views I respected immensely. Each of them is a voice in my life and each one is used by the Lord to form and refine me. The one whose opinion meant the most was (and still is) my husband, Paul. He has had a greater impact on my growth than anyone else. God uses him to train and mature me. Paul sees flaws and failings that I do not recognize and points them out in ways that enable me to change. Why am I saying this? I need these voices in my life. I need their direction and coaching but my reaction to their opinions was very wrong.

The Pattern

Let me paint a picture of one of my patterns. I am a preacher, so when I minister, I want to do it well. If my husband is present in the service, I am sensitive to his reactions. Sometimes I know that he is delighted by my message. Occasionally, I am not able to read the signs clearly. From time to time, I can sense his frustration. God showed me that when I felt his disappointment, I would feel as though Paul had removed his approval. This could cause me to crumple on the inside. I would feel as though his lack of approval meant that he now disapproved of me. It was unbearable. For years, these intense feelings came and went without me recognizing that there was an issue.

Then one weekend, about an hour before I was due to speak at the opening session of our church's annual women's conference, I "displeased" one of the three voices in my life. That telltale sinking sensation gripped me and I cried out to God. At the time, I could not work out if the timing of this misunderstanding was the devil's doing or if it was God! Was it a distraction or a revelation? As I opened my heart in the presence of the Lord, I suddenly saw the pattern in my life and I knew that the Spirit was at work. I gave every angst to the Lord and then went into the meeting to worship.

The Root

While I stood at the front of the auditorium in the presence of God, I inquired of the Lord. "If all is well, then why am I like this?" (Genesis 25:22b). I asked God why I struggled when any one of these three people was seemingly displeased with me. Almost immediately, God brought me back to two painful childhood memories. Both were to do with the way I was disciplined.

The first flashback was to a time when I was punished for not being perfect (or that is how it felt to me). I was beaten for not tidying away my shoes and then sent to my room where I cried alone for hours. My body was sore, but that was nothing compared to the desperate pain in my heart. I felt rejected. Intense loneliness filled my little heart. The Holy Spirit then reminded me of some words that were often said to me when I misbehaved. They made me feel ashamed and inadequate. They made me hate myself for failing. Fast forward forty years and the memories were still crystal clear. I fell to my knees and cried in the presence of God. I told Him how much these incidents hurt me. I poured out my pain and He poured in His healing.

Projecting Old Problems Onto New People

As the love of the Lord settled in my soul, I became aware of something significant. The occasional apparent removal of my husband's approval made me afraid that his love for me was in jeopardy. Let me make something clear. If you had asked me if I thought that my actions would dry up my husband's love, I would have said, "Of course not!" However, something inside me believed that if Paul did not approve of my *actions*, then he no longer approved of *me*. So I would be desperate to recover his affirmation.

As I reflected on what the Spirit of God revealed, I realized that I responded as though my husband's love was fickle and conditional. Secret fears whispered that my shortcomings might stifle his affections. Conditional love in my upbringing made me doubt my husband's feelings. The more I meditated, the crazier I realized it was. The same was true for the other two "voices" in my life. I had been subconsciously believing that their disapproval of something I did would cause them to remove their approval from me. I was believing lies and projecting childhood pain onto adult relationships. I was being controlled by subconscious fears. Notice that both childhood hurts were rooted in the way that I was corrected.

What About You?

Back to the annual women's conference... As I looked up from praying, the worship leader handed me the microphone. Whenever God does something in me, I know He wants to do it through me and sometimes that is instantly! Matthew 10:8 says, "Freely you have received, freely give..." I ministered on that very topic and the power of God invaded the room in an incredible way. Virtually every woman in attendance was affected to some extent. When the truth is revealed, we can be healed. Many captives were set free that night.

It is time to ask yourself if you suffer from similar issues... Think of someone whose opinions means a great deal to you. A person who you greatly admire and who you seek to emulate. Have you got someone in mind? Now imagine that you have done something that they do not like - something that irritates or disappoints them. How would you feel? Would the sense that their approval had been lifted make you churn on the inside? Would you feel the need to alleviate the inner discomfort and secure their pleasure once again?

Every time I have asked believers in meetings to consider this scenario, around 95 per cent of people have conceded that they struggle with an uncomfortable sense of disapproval. When people's praises provide our sense of approval then correction feels like rejection. When we know, deep down, that we are approved then we can handle feedback in all its forms. We do not need the approval of even the most influential people in our lives. So how can we get free once and for all?

Face The Facts

The first step is to face the truth. I encourage you to acknowledge before God that you get distressed when you sense you have displeased that all-important person. Work out how many folk have this effect on your emotions. For me, it was three. For you, it may be a greater or lesser number. It might be groups of individuals like leaders or teachers. Ephesians 5:13 in the Amplified says: "But when anything is exposed and reproved by the light, it is made visible and clear; and where everything is visible and clear there is light." Admit to God how you react in such situations.

Say Sorry

Fear of man is described in the Bible as a dangerous trap. An aversion to the removal of approval is a form of the fear of man. Fear is sin and fear always seeks to dictate our actions. For example, we may desperately try to please the person who is unimpressed. We could be overly apologetic. We might be eager to communicate to alleviate the distress, sending a flood of messages or trying to reach them on the phone. These are all examples of fear controlling our behavior. We end up doing what fear says, not what God wants. In fact, a lot of the time when we are churning, we are not even conscious of the Holy Spirit. It is for all these reasons that any time we succumb to fear, we need to apologize to the Lord. Galatians 1:10 in the NLT says, "Obviously, I'm not trying to win the approval of people, but of God. If pleasing people were my goal, I would not be Christ's servant." God is the One who validates. When we fear people, we have taken our eyes off the Lord.

Reveal The Root

It is easier to deal with unpleasant fruit when we have been healed at the root. Go to God and ask Him to expose any wounds in your heart. Just as I did, pray the prayer of Rebecca in Genesis 25:22b: "If all is well, then why am I like this?" Proverbs 20:27 says that the lamp of the Lord searches all the inner depths of our hearts. Ask the Holy Spirit to shine His light into your soul and uncover the buried pain that has led to this behavior. Perhaps you were disciplined terribly harshly as a child. Maybe you were cruelly chastised for not achieving at school. It could be that you were humiliated by peers or teachers for underperforming. Ask the Lord to reveal the reason.

Pour Out The Pain

If you have been shown the root cause, pour out your heart like water before the face of the Lord (Lamentations 2:19b). Tell Him what happened to you and how it made you feel. As we have learned through the chapters of this book, tell Him about every sadness. Explain what made you afraid. In the safety of your prayer closet, say the things you never said. Never hold back tears in the presence of the Lord. They release His healing in your heart. If you don't yet know why you react in the way you do, instead tell the Lord exactly how you feel any time approval is removed. Share with your Heavenly Father how horrible it feels and ask Him to heal your heart and set you free.

Cut It Off

Now that you have repented and received healing, it is time to make some decisions. I want to encourage you to renounce all forms of the fear of man in your life. If you have many struggles in this area, I want to encourage you to read my book Dreamstealers. There is a whole chapter in it on the fear of man. If this was a hidden issue - as it was for me - I want to persuade you to make a choice to change. Romans 12:2 in the New Living Translation says, "Be transformed by changing the way you think." It is time to evict the lies inside and allow the truth to affect your habits and behavior. We do not need to succumb to the spirit of fear. 2 Timothy 1:7 is clear: "For God has not given us a spirit of fear, but of power and of love and of a sound mind."

Fresh Focus

The approval of people will come and go. It is uncertain and often based upon circumstances. However, God's unconditional love means that even when He doesn't condone your actions, He approves of you. The meaning of the Greek word *dokimazo* is to examine, to test, to scrutinize. It means to recognize the genuine and deem it worthy. Not one of us is worthy without Jesus. We all fall short of the perfection of God. However, when Jesus died for us on the cross, He carried all our flaws and failings. He chose to take the blame for all our errors. When we receive Jesus as our Lord and Savior, all our wrongs are eradicated and we become blood-washed children of God. We become clean. We are attested and approved by God. 1 Thessalonians 2:4 says, "...we have been approved by God..."

The Lord of All has already approved you. If you have made Him your Lord, Jesus would vouch for you right now. One day, He will do so in heaven. He affirms your validity and places great value on you. You ARE approved by the Maker of heaven and earth. You cannot get better than that. Let this unchanging truth sink deep into your soul. Even if people around you falter, you have God's unwavering support. When you know in the depths of your heart that you have been endorsed in heaven, you will not cave in because of the removal of human approval. Let's pray.

Heavenly Father,

I am sorry for all the times when I have given in to fear. On occasion, I was more concerned about securing the approval of people than reminding myself of the value that You place on me. Forgive me, Lord. I have been preoccupied with pleasing (now tell God their name). Holy Spirit, shine Your light into my heart and show me why. Reveal any hurts deep within and heal my heart, oh Lord (If God has shown you the root, talk to Him in prayer. Tell Him what happened and how it made you feel. Pour out your pain.) Now heal me deep inside, I pray. I receive Your wonderful love. Thank You that You approve of me. Thank You that You delight in me. I am complete in You (Colossians 2:10).

From today, I renounce every form of man-pleasing. I do not seek the approval of people because I have already been approved by You, oh Lord. You approve of me. You have validated me. And I thank You with all of my heart.

In Jesus' name, I pray,

Amen.

Chapter 9
HOW HARD CAN IT BE?

We live in a world of marketing. According to the ads, if you use the hairspray, you will get the guy. A woman sprays her hair, skips downstairs, bounces out of her door and onto the street where she runs into the adoring arms of her handsome hunk. Washing powders don't just guarantee wonderfully white washing. The storylines suggest that we may even get the picture perfect family too! We are surrounded by great marketing which gives us a myriad of reasons why we should try, buy, rent and borrow.

This is not a new idea. Have you ever noticed that most effective success strategies can be found in Scripture? To me, God is the ultimate marketeer. He is a good, good Father who seeks to explain and promote the benefits of obedience and expose the real risks of rebellion. Through His Word, He tries to motivate us to do the right things. He gives us instructions to protect us from doing the wrong things.

God's Deal Breaker

We are going to look at one particular heart issue that is a deal breaker for God. This matter of the heart has the capacity to keep you out of your 'promised land'. Your promised land is the dream deep inside that you long to see unfold. Your promised land is your highest potential, your greatest purpose and deepest desire. God wants it for you more than you do. His plans for you are to prosper you, to give you a hope and a bright future. However, there is a heart attitude that can spoil everything.

Psalm 95:7b-11 reads: "Today, if you will hear His voice: 'Do not harden your hearts, as in the rebellion, as in the day of trial in the wilderness, when your fathers tested Me; they tried Me, though they saw My work. For forty years I was grieved with that generation, and said, "It is a people who go astray in their hearts, and they do not know My ways." So I swore in My wrath, 'They shall not enter My rest.'"

This is one of Scripture's saddest passages. The children of Israel hardened their hearts. It grieved God to such an extent that He made an irrevocable decision to keep them from their promised land. We can make mistakes that have consequences. This was different. This heart attitude hurt our Heavenly Father so much that He barred His beloved children from their original inheritance.

Cold & Closed

What do we mean by hardness of heart? Later in this chapter, we will unpack it in more detail. For now, I want to give you a very simple definition. At its core, a hard heart is a cold, closed heart. It is unfeeling, jaded and somewhat callous. I could have a hard heart towards God or towards people. In Exodus, the children of Israel became hard towards the Lord. When times were tough, they doubted God's goodness and refused to remember the miracles of yesterday. That grieved the Father. In Deuteronomy 15:7, we are warned not to close our hearts towards particular people: "...you shall not harden your heart nor shut your hand from your poor brother...". Whichever way it rears its ugly head, a hard heart puts me at risk of harming myself and, at the same time, of hurting God.

So how does a heart harden? It is simple really. Life - with all its difficulties and disappointments - happens. There is a famous passage in the Bible where we see God go so far as to conduct transplants: "... I will take the heart of stone out of your flesh and give you a heart of flesh." (Ezekiel 36:26b). The hearts of His people had become so stony that He had to take them through major surgery to replace their hardness with His tenderness. Earlier verses in this chapter provide some clues about the origins of this hardness.

Ezekiel 36:3 says, "...They made you desolate and swallowed you up on every side, so that you became the possession of the rest of the nations, and you are taken up by the lips of talkers and slandered by the people." This is a painful picture of rejection, humiliation, control and mockery. This one verse describes the terrible trials that these people endured. They were isolated, abused and ridiculed. I don't know what has happened to you. I do know that the enemy hates you and is hell-bent on your demise. Maybe you have been treated like a doormat by people who were supposed to take care of you. Perhaps you have been let down by someone you held in high esteem. You may have been publicly humiliated. Whatever you have experienced, I know that it must have hurt. The enemy's plan for your pain is to cause you to close your heart. He knows that if he can make you shut down, he is a step nearer to getting you to harden completely.

Hurt & Hard

Job 5:7 says that just as sparks fly upwards, so man is born to trouble. Have you ever seen a blacksmith at work? In Britain, when there is a general election, all our politicians are filmed visiting factories. They are presenting a picture to the voting world that they are in touch with the people. They always seem to visit workshops where specialists are molding metal. We see a shower of sparks as the iron is shaped. They always fly upwards! In other words, the Bible is warning us that just as surely as sparks fly upwards, so you and I are going to go through really tough times.

People are going to be cruel (and they probably already have been). Friends are going to forsake you (and maybe you are feeling that pain right now). Family members will fail you and loved ones will let you down. The natural reaction is to recoil. Perhaps you have pulled away from people and withdrawn. The danger is that we can become closed and cold. That is why we all need to be healed. The more you allow the Lord to heal your hurts as they happen, the easier it will be to keep your heart tender.

Broken In Church

Richard got saved as an eight year old child. By his teenage years, he was enthusiastically serving in church. Passionate for Jesus, Richard spent all his spare time attending meetings and gave every penny of his pocket money in the offerings. He became a leader.

As a conscientious young man, Richard knew it was also important to excel in his school studies. One particular weekend, just before a major exam, there was a leadership meeting at church. He contacted the pastor and explained that he would be unable to attend because of his forthcoming test. To Richard's shock, he was told that because of his 'disloyalty', he had been thrown out of the leadership team. He was just 18 years of age at the time. It was like a punch in the guts. Richard felt betrayed, bewildered and heartbroken.

Let's fast-forward 30 years. Richard never stopped loving Jesus, but he was now somewhat wary of churches. He would attend meetings and serve out of loyalty to the Lord. However, deep down he felt afraid of commitment. During a Healed for Life meeting, God shone His light into Richard's heart. Although he knew his own history, he had no idea why he always felt so wary.

As one of the team prayed for this dear man, he broke and wept. He had no idea he was still wounded deep within. He poured out his pain like water before the face of the Lord and God healed his heart. Afterwards, as he rested in God's presence, a love for the church welled up inside. He realized that for more than two decades, hurt had kept his heart hard towards the church. Now he was healed, his heart became tender. He was free to love the body of Christ. That man is now a leader in Healed for Life, bringing freedom to many.

God Is Bothered

When you read the second half of Ezekiel 36, you discover just how much it hurts God when we are wounded. When He saw the suffering of Israel, He became angry and determined to pay back those who had distressed His people. Not only that, the Lord put together a plan to bring them relief and restoration. However, His people recoiled in their pain, closed the doors of their hearts and turned their backs on God (see Ezekiel 36:17). If you're reading this book, you have probably not walked away from the Lord. It may be that you have distanced yourself from people who have wounded you. Of course there are times when doing this is wise. All too often, it is a defense mechanism to avoid any more harm. It is true that God gave us guards for our hearts (see Proverbs

115

4:23). However, the purpose of our protective shutters is to keep us from damage - not to stop us loving.

The enemy wants you to shut down when you are wounded. The devil whispers lies in your ears, suggesting that God is there for others, but is missing in action over your life. This could not be further from the truth. The Lord loves you and has a plan for your restoration and fulfillment. He wants to heal you of every hurt so that you can love and trust again.

How Hard Is Your Heart?

Let's go back to Psalm 95. Verse 8 says, "Do not harden your hearts, as in the rebellion." The Hebrew word *meribah* that has been translated as rebellion actually means strife or quarrel. It is very easy for us to harden our hearts when we are feeling stressed or argumentative. It might be strife at home or contention at church. Perhaps there has been a misunderstanding between you and a brother or an argument with a leader. Strife is a breeding ground for hardness of heart.

Hardness of heart is like yeast: it often grows. What do I mean? In the story of the conflict between Pharaoh and Moses, we see the Egyptian leader's heart slowly but surely set like stone. Three times Scripture says, "And Pharaoh's heart grew hard..." (e.g. Exodus 7:13), twice it says, "...he hardened his heart..." (e.g. Exodus 8:15) and once we read, "...neither was his heart moved..." (Exodus 7:23). Eventually the Bible states: "So the heart of Pharaoh was hard..." (Exodus 9:35). It is a slippery slope and the tougher we become the more difficult it is to be tender again. Let us be aware of how hard we are on the inside - both towards God and the people around us.

Picture a door to your heart and think about your relationship with a destiny friend. It starts with that door wide open towards that person. Maybe you go through a trying time and strife creeps into your relationship. You get annoyed and close it a little. They do something thoughtless and you close it a little further. The next time you meet up, there is a strain between you. They do not call. Now the door is only slightly ajar. All it takes is a final mis-understanding and you slam the door of your heart shut towards that person.

The Power Of Relationships

Throughout the Bible, God used relationships to bring His purposes to pass. The Lord had a great plan for Abraham to become a father of multitudes but it would only be fulfilled through His relationship with Sarah. Lot prospered as long as he was connected to Abraham. Pharaoh's butler opened the door for Joseph's promotion from prisoner to prime minister. Mordecai's wise advice carved out the pathway for Esther to become queen.

Your destiny is wrapped up in your divine relationships. There are probably four or five people who are pivotal to you fulfilling your purpose. The enemy will target those relationships first. He wants you to harden your heart towards your spouse, your leader, your prayer partner, your brother or your sister: the very people who will help you to achieve your potential.

We all know the saying that opposites attract. In truth, I believe that God puts people in our path who have the gifts or character attributes that we need to develop. He will not normally send someone to you who is the same as you. He will send you a mentor or a friend who is strong where you are weak. Now that may also mean that you have strengths that they lack. Stop and think about this for a while. It can be hard to follow a leader whose weaknesses you can see. Yet they may be the exact person you need to open the door to your destiny. I encourage you to take your eyes off their shortcomings and instead thank God for the blessing that these people are in your life.

Different Is Not Wrong!

For the first few years of our marriage, Paul and I would often clash over our dreams. I absolutely love vacations. Any time we have any spare money, my mind immediately drifts across the seas to secluded sandy beaches. I love holidays! However, my husband thinks they are a terrible waste. He, on the other hand, loves watches. I cannot understand why anyone would rather tell the time than pass the time together in a distant land. This would cause great consternation. That is, until we both decided we wanted to make each other happy instead. What's my point? You are probably very different to the people who can help you reach your purpose. That does not mean they are wrong for you. It definitely does not mean we should close our hearts towards them. It simply means we need to practice love and humility on the way.

The devil wants to bring strife into your divine relationships because he wants you to harden your heart towards the very people you need. Jesus said to Peter, "Satan has asked for you, that he may sift you as wheat..." (Luke 22:31). When you sift flour, for example, you separate the clumps. The devil was trying to separate Peter from the other disciples because he wanted to cut him off from his mandate. The enemy has no new tricks. He will try to harden your heart towards the very people God provided to help you reach your promised land.

Satan succeeded in cutting off many of the Israelites by using the same trick: "They made their hearts as hard as flint and would not listen to the... words that the Lord Almighty had sent by his Spirit through the earlier prophets." Zechariah 7:12 (NIV) A prophet is someone who brings the word of the Lord. These children of Israel closed their hearts to the very people God was using to give them direction. It cost them their destiny.

Marriage

In the Gospels, Jesus explained why Moses introduced divorce. It was not because of unfaithfulness, although the Bible clearly states that adultery is grounds for legal separation. Divorce became necessary because of hardness of heart: "He said to them, 'Moses, because of the hardness of your hearts, permitted you to divorce your wives, but from the beginning it was not so.'" Matthew 19:8. If you have been hurt in marriage, please do not shut this book. I will share how God wants to heal your heart. But first, I want to address this pivotal issue. If you are married or would like to be, stop for a moment and ask the Holy Spirit to give you revelation about this point before you read on...

God's plan for marriage is that it gets better every year. Despite many painful struggles, I can honestly say that I love my husband Paul more now than ever before. I know that he would say the same about me. People often say marriage is hard work. I believe that developing a genuinely rewarding relationship is a lot of heart work. I think that one of the greatest keys to a wonderful relationship is to keep your heart tender towards your spouse. I list five symptoms of a hard heart later in this chapter. They are followed by the five fixes to protect our tenderness. I encourage you to rethink your relationship with your spouse in the light of those points. They could be the keys that save your marriage.

It is not always the big issues. The Bible says the small foxes spoil the vine... Recently, Paul and I were returning from a visit to the north of England. It was a long drive and the roads were very busy. The atmosphere in our car was not great. My husband was tired and I was crabby, to say the least. It seemed that everything he said was irritating me. I could feel my heart trying to harden. Repeatedly, I had to pull myself back from coldness and re-route myself towards tenderness. It is an act of the will, but it is well worth the effort.

When Things Fall Apart

Every breakdown in marriage produces at least two casualties. There are usually many more. If you have been wounded in wedlock, God wants to heal your heart. Most of us embark on marriage believing it will be forever. So as well as breaking hearts, separation shatters dreams. Usually, there will be a need for a powerful mix of healing and forgiveness.

The Road to Recovery

After 37 years of marriage, Angela went through a devastating divorce. Her husband had been abusive and unfaithful. He had withheld money from her. She felt humiliated, heartbroken and was on the verge of a breakdown. Angela's agony turned to bitterness and hate. Pastors, friends and family tried to persuade her, but she found it impossible to forgive. She wanted revenge and longed for something terrible to happen to him.

Angela was given a copy of my book 'Lifting the Mask'. Hope grew in her heart. When she read how God healed me after the death of our daughter, she began to believe that He could restore her too. Angela allowed the love of the Lord to flood into her heart and wash away anguish and pain. She opened up deep inside to God's supernatural love. She realized that unforgiveness was hurting her more than him. She made a difficult, but firm decision. Angela forgave her husband from the depths of her heart. It took time, yet she relinquished her right to retaliation and gave up her desire for his demise. Making every effort to let go, she released that man into God's hands.

For the first time in many years, Angela experienced real peace and genuine joy. Some months later, she bumped into her ex-husband at a family function. Walking towards him, she reached out her hand and greeted him warmly. The look of shock on his face was a picture. Angela was happy and free.

Let's Learn From Jesus

Even a man in Jesus' inner circle suffered from a hard heart so we should not be surprised if we struggle to maintain a right attitude at times. Perhaps Thomas became a bit too familiar and forgot who it was he was following. As a result, he doubted his friend (and master!) while others believed. As I am married to him, it might be easy for me to take the gift that my pastor husband carries for granted. Yet every time he preaches, there is something in it for me. I deliberately approach his ministry with great expectation and I am rarely disappointed. Familiarity causes us to close up on the inside. It is a form of hardness and it limits what we receive from our Heavenly Father because He works through people.

Shortly after Jesus fed the 5,000, the disciples and their Master embarked on a boat trip. Once on board, the 12 realized that they had forgotten to bring bread and were worried about what to eat. Jesus reprimanded them - not because of their mistake, but because of the state of their hearts. He described five symptoms of hardness. Let's read Mark 8:17-18, "But Jesus... said to them, 'Why do you reason because you have no bread? Do you not yet perceive nor understand? Is your heart still hardened? Having eyes, do you not see? And having ears, do you not hear? And do you not remember?'" These symptoms apply to us, whether we are cold towards God or towards people. As you read the shortcomings below, allow the Holy Spirit to search your heart. When we are aware of our failings, we can change.

Symptoms of a Hardening Heart

1. We don't perceive - we don't get the big picture and instead get bogged down in inconsequential details. We are not aware of what the enemy is trying to do or what God would love to do. Our minds are blurred.

2. We don't understand - we are only thinking about our own issues. We are wanting to be understood instead of seeking to understand. We don't appreciate the spiritual realm or see what is going on from an eternal perspective.

3. We don't see - we cannot spot what is happening in someone else's life. We are blinded to their issues and we see only our own challenges. We are not looking with the eyes of faith at what God could do.

4. We don't hear - our friend may be talking but we cannot really hear what they are saying. We are more concerned with explaining than listening. We are not listening to God's voice either.

5. We don't remember - we do not remember all the reasons why we loved them in the first place. We do not remember the blessings of God or His goodness in our lives.

Five Fixes

If you know you need to soften your heart towards God, look at the list above and do the opposite. 1) Recognize that the enemy is seeking to cut you off from the blessings of obedience. 2) Ask for a heavenly perspective of your situation. 3) See the goodness of God in your life and ask the Spirit to open your eyes to what He is doing for you behind the scenes. 4) Listen to what the Lord is saying in this season. 5) Finally, but possibly most importantly, think back and remember all the good things that God has done for you. Stop and thank Him from the bottom of your heart for every blessing in your life.

Close The Door To The Devil

Let's look now at how we deal with hardness towards others. It might be a spouse, a fiancé, a leader or a teacher. It could be a brother, a sister or a friend. Remember, God uses people to get you ready for and positioned to fulfill your purpose. Fully aware of this, satan tries to separate you from your destiny connectors. Ask the Holy Spirit right now to show you if you are harboring any hardness towards anyone. Once you know what you're dealing with, we will look at how you can boot the devil out of your relationships. Here are five fixes:

1. Put yourself in their shoes - ask yourself what pressures they may be facing. Remember to think about the big picture. Is this really important in the grand scheme of things? Ask yourself what God might be doing right now in you through them.

2. Try to understand - we all long to be understood by someone. Maybe even the very people with whom we are upset. Yet the Bible teaches us to seek to understand. Proverbs 2:2 says, "...Apply your heart to understanding..." When we apply ourselves to something, we give it our full attention and make every effort. We should seek to understand the people that we feel like shutting out of our lives. We can ask God for His heart towards them so that we grow in empathy. Solomon asked for understanding and the Bible says that God gave him a very big heart. When we understand - despite every opportunity to judge - it is a sign of generosity of spirit.

3. See what is at stake - ask the Holy Spirit to open your eyes so that you can see what satan is doing. Acknowledge that the enemy has been at work. If you have swallowed the devil's lies, say sorry to God. Then remind yourself of God's purposes for this relationship.

4. Hear what they are saying - listen carefully with an open mind and a tender heart to what that person is saying. Also, follow the leading of the Holy Spirit. Ask Him to give you wisdom.

5. Remember the best - this is the key! Remember all the reasons why you loved them in the first place. Right there, you will feel your heart softening and hopefully you will even start smiling! Remind yourself why God connected you. Think back to all the times that the Lord has used them in one way or another to bless you. Thank God for their life and your relationship.

Transplant Time

Remember where we started. Hard hearts can shut heaven's doors. I want God to tenderize my heart and I am sure that you do too. I want Him to expose any hardness so that I can repent and change. I long for Him to take out my stony heart and give me a heart of flesh. I believe there are two steps towards tenderness.

1. God's Part

Doing transplants is God's role. He wants to meet you and I in a supernatural encounter. In His precious presence, He can change even the hardest of hearts. Just as He heals, He can also soften. We only need to be open and willing. If you desire for God to take away the old and give you a brand new beginning, He will do that for you. Surrender yourself anew to Him. Allow the Lord to access every area of your heart and life. Give Him permission to give you a new heart that is after His heart.

2. Our Part

As we have already discussed, the soul is made up of the mind, the will and the emotions. Many of the issues that we have addressed in this book relate to the emotions. However, hardness of heart is a matter of the will. We can choose to soften our hearts towards both God and people. It is our decision whether we shut down and withdraw or if we open up and show love. Thankfully, the Holy Spirit is our helper and will support us all the way. Let's pray...

Heavenly Father,

I realize that my heart has been hard. I have been closed and cold towards **(Now tell God who you have been hard-hearted towards. Explain what you did, felt or said that was wrong)**. *Please forgive me, Lord. Not only have I wronged them, but I have also wronged You. I am so sorry, Lord. Thank You for placing the right people in my life. From this day forth, I will seek to value and honor them.*

At times, I have also been hard-hearted towards You, oh Lord. I have not remembered Your goodness to me. I have too quickly forgotten the miracles You have done in my life. I am so sorry, Lord. Please forgive me.

I ask You to take out my stony heart. Oh Lord, please remove my hardness and coldness. Melt my icy reactions and soften me from the inside out. Change me, oh Lord. I pray that You may be glorified in me.

I make a choice today to walk in love. I will seek to understand. I will put myself in other people's shoes. I will seek to see things from a different perspective. I will look for the good in others. I remember all the reasons why I loved these people in the first place. Holy Spirit, please help me to make daily choices that will please You. Please help me to maintain a tender heart towards You and my "destiny connectors".

In Jesus' name, I pray,

Amen

Chapter 10
YOUR INNER INTERPRETER

I often have encounters with God at 30,000 feet! No, not up a mountain, but while I am in an airplane. A while back, as I was flying to America, I was praying and asking the Lord to refresh my heart. I had been feeling weary so I brought every care to Him in prayer. Afterwards, I was still aware of some sadness beneath the surface. I did not know why so I sought the Lord and asked Him (once again), "If all is well, then why am I like this?" Almost instantly, the Spirit of God revealed to me that I was believing the lie that life was tough and hard. I was astonished. It was true.

You see, I had been working very hard for months establishing our ministry in America. Bringing Healed for Life to the US was not easy. The enemy hates this ministry because people become their best, marriages and families are restored and churches get built. As a result, the devil tried to oppose us at every turn. However, God is always faithful and that year was no exception. He had opened doors and shown me favor. He had blessed me and refreshed me in His presence over and over again.

I repented immediately and then declared the truth to myself: "Life is good!" Almost immediately, every source of sadness dissipated and joy filled my heart. I worshipped the Lord and enjoyed my new-found freedom. Then the Lord showed me that this is a common problem among God's people.

The Lie

We believe all sorts of lies! Some creep in by a process of osmosis. Things happen around us and we draw inaccurate conclusions. People may say things that sow negative seeds in our souls. The general atmosphere of the world influences our attitudes and opinions. Some lies are rooted in soul wounds. If you have been treated like a second class citizen, you may end up believing that you are inferior. If your parents only praised you when you succeeded, you might believe the lie that your value is based on your ability. If you were abused, you may think that you are dirty. If a teacher put you down, you may assume that you are stupid.

As we have already learned, the Bible is clear that our hearts have a weakness in the form of deception and lies. Jeremiah 17:9-10 says, "The heart is deceitful above all things, and desperately wicked; who can know it? I, the Lord, search the heart, I test the mind, even to give every man according to his ways, according to the fruit of his doings." The first point from this passage is that the human heart is deceitful. Just as it is capable of love and romance and heartbreak and pain, so your heart can - and probably does - lie to you. Sometimes we deny the truth because it is too painful or uncomfortable. Rather than acknowledging that I'm an oversensitive wife, I would rather believe that I have an insensitive husband! The truth challenges, humbles and hurts so we often settle instead for a lie. At other times, our hearts believe lies that we are told. Either way, it is vital that we admit our hearts need help.

The Heart's Default

Have you ever grabbed a shopping cart at the store only to find that the trolley you chose had a wonky wheel? If you are anything like me, you will then have spent all your time walking through the aisles trying desperately to keep the cart straight. You missed the groceries you needed because your trolley diverted your attention and the wonky wheel kept pulling you to one side. Its default was to turn to the left or the right. That is what Jeremiah 17:19 is telling us that the human heart is like. We have a default towards deception, a tendency to believe lies. We have to work hard to keep our hearts from veering into deception or denial.

The second part of our passage shows the Holy Spirit's response to our heart problems. The Lord searches and evaluates what is going on inside. He longs for us to face the truth so that we can be free. He will not settle for superficial responses to deep issues. I like the way the Message version of the Bible expresses Jeremiah 17:10: "But I, God, search the heart and examine the mind. I get to the heart of the human. I get to the root of things. I treat them as they really are, not as they pretend to be."

The Interpreter

If you believe a lie, then you will interpret everything that happens through that lie. For example, if I believe the lie that my life is tough, then I will interpret everything that occurs through that lie. Just a few hours after God revealed that I had been believing the lie that life was hard, I landed in Miami. As I switched my phone back on, I received a text from the lady who was due to pick me up. She explained that she had a problem with her car. If I had still been believing the lie, I would have seen that situation as further evidence that life was hard. Instead, my heart went out to this lady and I hoped her vehicle would be repaired quickly. With joy in my heart, I stopped for a coffee and then ordered a taxi.

We run a bilingual version of our two day course Healed for Life. During one session, I was sharing with painful honesty about some old issues in my marriage. I explained that the most important moment was when I faced the truth. I no longer blamed my husband for all our problems and recognized that my shortcomings were the cause of our issues. Somehow the interpreter did not catch what I said. Soon there was uproar in the auditorium. It became clear that my interpreter had said that the root of our problems was that my husband was a womanizer! I cleared up the mistake, we all roared with laughter and I carried on. What is my point? The Spanish speakers believed that the interpreter was telling the truth – until we cleared up the misunderstanding. It was the only version of the story that they could hear. It is the same for you and me. We believe our inner interpreter is presenting an accurate account of events. We take what it says as gospel.

Even Great Men Believe Lies

At the start of his ministry, I believe that Moses had an inner interpreter. Let me set the scene. The people of Israel were horribly oppressed by their Egyptian taskmasters and desperate for deliverance. They cried out to God who heard their prayers. The Lord developed a plan and chose a leader who would set His people free. Moses was God's man for the job. However, at the start of his ministry, Moses had a problem. He believed a lie that nearly cost him his destiny and Israel's deliverance. Moses interpreted everything he heard through the filter which said: "I'm not qualified".

Perhaps he believed he was too old. Who has heard of an old age pensioner pioneering a movement, he might have thought. Maybe Moses' sense of inadequacy was rooted in guilt. He had murdered a man out of anger 40 years earlier. Who would want a former killer to lead a nation? It could have been his clumsy communication skills that made him doubt his suitability. Why would anyone want to follow a leader with a lisp or a stammer?

I'm Not Qualified!

Let's look at the story in Scripture. In Exodus 3:10-11, God shared his plan with Moses: "I am sending you to Pharaoh to bring my people the Israelites out of Egypt. Moses replied to God, 'Who am I that I should go to Pharaoh and bring the Israelites out of Egypt?'" His first reaction was not a sense of privilege at having been picked. His inner interpreter was whispering, "You're not qualified!" Moses was horrified at the idea of leading. He felt inadequate.

God promised that He would use Moses in amazing ways. The Lord reassured Moses that the leaders of Israel would listen to him and that He Himself would guide him all the way. No matter what God said, Moses's inner interpreter had an answer: "...They won't believe me..." (Exodus 4:1) and "...I can't speak well..." (Exodus 4:10). All the way through, Moses was hearing his heart say, "You're not qualified!" Finally, Moses pleaded with God to send someone else (Exodus 4:13).

How many times do we try to sidestep our way out of the purposes of God because we do not think that we have what it takes? Perhaps you believe that you are God's back-up plan or His second choice. You think you will fulfill the role until someone more suitable arrives to take your place.

Rosie helped out with the worship at a brand new church. She knew that it was not her main gifting, but at the same time the presence of God turned up whenever she led. She put her heart and soul into it because she had always been a worshipper. Then one month, when the rotation was being circulated, she noticed that her name had been removed. A talented singer had joined the congregation and stepped into the breach. Although Rosie knew that it was right for her to step down, she felt rejected because no one spoke to her about the situation.

Exposing The Enemy

Rosie moved on and gave little thought to those events. Nevertheless, she started to believe a deep-seated lie: "I'm Plan B." She had no idea that this experience had marked her. However, for the next twenty years, despite her heartfelt love for God, Rosie always treated ministry with caution. She never gave her best, just in case she was deselected. She was greatly gifted and loved the Lord, but always held back.

At Healed for Life, God shone His light into her heart. She realized for the first time how much she had been hurt all those years earlier. Rosie told the Lord that she felt discarded. She poured out her pain and He healed her heart. She realized that she had been believing the devil's lie and God revealed the truth that she was His choice. For the first time in two decades, she felt free. Rosie returned to her home church and gave her very best to God. She is now part of their senior leadership team and runs a successful, multifaceted evangelism and outreach department.

Let us return to the story of Moses. In the end, he recognized that he was believing a lie and went on to lead with great confidence. He realized deep down that God had called him and would always equip him. How many others live their lives believing a myriad of untruths? You may see life through the lie that I believed - life is hard. That assertion will sap your strength and gag your gratitude. Perhaps your Inner Interpreter works according to the notion that 'life is not fair'. When something good happens to someone else, you easily feel cheated. When good gifts come your way, you assume they will be removed soon. You think your lot is harder, worse or simply more complicated than everyone else's.

What's Your Story?

Maybe you are convinced that you are not good enough. Perhaps you experienced pain in childhood that imprinted this myth across the tablet of your heart. Maybe you assume that you are stupid. Words were spoken that crushed your confidence and caused you to draw this false conclusion. It could be that you think that you are not lovable. Repeated rejections have led you to suppose that you are not what other people want. Some untruths - like that one - are foul and brutal. God wants to expose the lie, heal any wounds in your heart and lead you into the truth.

If you believe a lie, your Inner Interpreter will translate life in the light of that lie. The enemy aims to steal your joy and limit your growth. Ephesians 5:13 says: "Anything exposed to the light becomes visible..." This means that when we allow the light of God's word to shine on the issues of our hearts, our errors become obvious. When we know that there is a problem, it is easy to get free. As soon as the Holy Spirit exposed the fable that I had been believing, it lost its power. Then the truth that life is a joy set me free. When the Holy Spirit reveals a deception, He also provides the counteracting truth that will set you up for success. Let's pray.

Heavenly Father,

I realize that I have been believing the lie that (now tell God what untruth you have taken as truth.) I realize that it is a lie! I ask You to reveal any root that produced the fruit of this lie. (If the Holy Spirit has revealed any hidden hurts, tell Him what was said or done and how it made you feel. Pour out your pain in His presence and ask Him to heal your heart.) I will no longer believe the enemy. Instead, I believe Your word. (Now ask the Lord to give you a verse that confirms His truth about your old lie.) Thank You, Lord, for revealing Your word to my heart. I stand on Your word, which is forever settled. I give You all the glory.

In Jesus' name, I pray,

Amen.

Chapter 11
THE WHOLE ARMOR OF SATAN

The enemy is not capable of original thought. He is not creative. The devil just copies what God does and develops harmful counterfeits of kingdom principles. For example, the Lord created a substance called faith and placed it in the hearts of His people. Faith is believing what God says and it is the currency of heaven. By faith, we lay hold of the promises in the Bible. The devil's counterfeit is fear. Satan sows fear into the hearts of God's people. Fear is believing the enemy's threats and it is the currency of hell. Fear holds us captive.

Another example is conviction: God's mechanism for leading us away from wrongdoing and into righteous living. Conviction comes from the Holy Spirit and it creates a desire to do the right thing. It woos us away from sin and into the arms of the Father. The devil's counterfeit is condemnation. It binds God's people up in guilt and makes them turn away in shame from the Father. Condemnation tells a person that their shortcomings have disqualified them. It leaves people feeling hopeless.

The Kit

The book of Ephesians famously describes the armor that God gives His people. We are in a war so we need to be equipped to fight the enemy and defend ourselves when we are under attack. The armor of God enables us to stand strong in every storm and win life's battles. Jesus modeled the wearing of armor. In Isaiah 59:17, we see the Redeemer clothing Himself with some of the garments He instructed us to put on in the New Testament.

"Therefore take up the whole armor of God, that you may be able to withstand in the evil day, and having done all, to stand. Stand therefore, having girded your waist with truth, having put on the breastplate of righteousness, and having shod your feet with the preparation of the gospel of peace; above all, taking the shield of faith with which you will be able to quench all the fiery darts of the wicked one. And take the helmet of salvation, and the sword of the Spirit, which is the word of God..." Ephesians 6:13-17

God's armor is vital for us to live in victory. It enables us to grow and thrive in every area of life. We need His armor to live as Christian soldiers. I believe that the enemy has developed counterfeits of the whole armor of God. While the Lord's security clothing is there to protect and equip, the devil's accessories are designed to harm and hinder. Satan wants to stop you succeeding by tricking you into holding beliefs and maintaining behavior that will keep you bound.

We are going to look at the devil's dirty devices. Once we recognize his counterfeits, we will be empowered to strip off his kit and kick him out of our lives!

Belt Up - with Truth or Lies?

The Bible tells us to gird ourselves with the belt of truth. A belt holds up your pants and protects your dignity. We may think that by hiding the truth we protect our privacy. However, it does not work that way. Uncomfortable secrets are satan's ammunition. According to Ephesians 5:13, whatever we bring into the light becomes light. The only sin that is a problem is unconfessed sin. When we say sorry to the Lord, all our iniquities and errors are washed clean by the blood of Jesus. Truth before the Lord enables us to stand strong without guilt or shame. Truth protects our greatest vulnerabilities. That is why it is a belt.

Proverbs 23:23 tells us that the truth comes at a price: "Buy the truth and do not sell it." We have already discussed the fact that the truth can be costly. Sometimes it hurts. If I think that I am kind and patient but discover that most people find me harsh and touchy, it can be painful to face reality. However, truth paves the way for transformation and freedom.

Bitter Pill

A while back, my husband and I were walking in the beautiful British countryside. We had taken a much needed day off and were enjoying some time together. As we strolled through the woods, we were chatting about my dearest friend, Larissa. Out of the blue, Paul piped up: "Larissa should get a medal. You're horribly domineering towards her!" (You need to understand something, I have exactly the husband God knew I would need. He tells me the truth because he wants me to become my best). I reeled at the remark and then paused for thought. The devil would have loved it if I had argued, but I have learned that defensiveness is pointless. Don't get me wrong. My flesh would have preferred to believe the lie that my husband was misguided and mean. I would have loved to lash back like I always used to, but I wanted to grow. So after quiet reflection, I sheepishly concluded that he might be right. The truth was a painful pill to swallow, yet it helped me to become a better version of myself.

Marked By Mistakes

The enemy wants us to tie a belt of deception around our waists. He likes us to believe lies about ourselves and other people. The lies about ourselves are crafted to keep us confined and condemned. The devil will tell you that you are permanently marked by your mistakes and disqualified from promotion. The enemy promotes lies and then tells us to be afraid of the truth. He wants you to dread your past being uncovered. The devil wants you to duck, dive and hide. He wants you to cover any shame under a shroud of untruths.

Let me show you how the enemy handles your secrets. He holds them like bullets in a gun. Every time you think you might be found out, it is as though satan holds that gun to your head - loaded with your uncomfortable memories. Remember, the devil is the father of lies. Jesus paid the price for all our flaws and failings. When we expose our errors to the light, they become light. You do not need to tell the world about every mistake you ever made. However, at the same time, you should not be concerned if they are exposed. When we bring our past into the open, it loses its power. It is like taking that gun from the devil, firing every one of those bullets into the air and then handing him back an empty weapon. Lies don't protect, they torment.

I'm Fine!

On the other hand, satan wants us to believe that we are fine when we really need God's help. The belt of deception causes us to ignore our pain and cover up our shortcomings. It leads us to be dishonest about the state of our lives for fear of being thought a fraud. The belt of deception makes us carry on, even when everything is falling apart on the inside.

Lies About Others

Lies about others can keep us suspicious so that we separate ourselves from the very people who could help us. Perhaps someone has said something that sowed doubt in your heart about the motives of family or friends. Maybe you heard a rumor or believed an accusation. Before we know it, we are backing away from brothers or sisters who were once a great blessing. The belt of deception is destructive.

Bulletproof Vest - of Righteousness or Self-righteousness?

A breastplate was vital to a soldier's safety as it protected his heart. It was the bulletproof vest of Roman army uniforms. The breastplate in God's armor is righteousness. Thanks to the blood of Jesus, we are forgiven of our sins. According to Scripture we are made completely clean before God. Jesus was punished for every sin we ever committed. Our sins are not just forgiven, they are taken away. It is just as if you never sinned. But it does not stop there. The Bible says that we are the righteousness of God in Christ Jesus. An exchange took place at the cross. Jesus took our sinfulness and swapped it for His righteousness.

So how does satan warp this one? The enemy aims to infect our hearts by tempting us into a sense of self-righteousness. This can present itself in two almost opposing ways. For some, satan seeks to make us feel superior to others because of our own efforts. The Bible says that my righteousness is like filthy rags to the Lord (Isaiah 64:6). However, the enemy wants us to feel proud of our own efforts. Remember that the devil lost absolutely everything because of pride. He had it all - power, privilege and position - and yet he threw it all away because he became impressed with himself. As a result, the enemy is always looking to trip us up with the exact same sin. It can be subtle, yet it is a slippery slope that takes our eyes off our wonderful Savior. Nothing I own and nothing I have achieved was by my might or power. Everything good in my life was made possible by His Holy Spirit.

Sometimes, satan spins this one differently. If he knows that you have more of a tendency towards condemnation than pride or arrogance, he may tell you that you do not qualify for the righteousness of God. The devil may deceive you into believing that your filthy rags could never be washed clean. The sad truth is that this is just the other side of the same lie. It suggests that the blood of Jesus is not enough for you, that somehow your sin is greater than His sacrifice. This mindset is still based on self-justification. Once again, we think we have to rely upon our own works to be made holy. The truth is that the blood of Jesus is more powerful than any flaw or failing known to man. It is all-powerful.

Suited and Booted - with the Gospel or Gossip?

When we have got our shoes on, we are ready to go. God wants us to be suited and booted, prepared to share His story and our testimony. The more He does in us, the more He can do through us. Jesus told His team, "Freely you have received, freely give." I want to encourage you. Your testimony is the most meaningful message you can preach. As God heals your heart and turns your life around, share your journey with your nearest and dearest. Friends and family might not realize that they need Jesus. However, most folk know that their hearts hurt. No one escapes the scrapes of life. When you share how God restored you, you may well be amazed at how many people will open up and listen.

We were designed with a desire to identify with others. We were formed for fellowship because we were made in God's image. Sharing with others is natural. Before I go any further, I would like to pick up on an important point. If you back away from forming friendships or clam up when others freely communicate, I encourage you to ask God why. Isolation was never God's plan for any of His people. It is the enemy who promotes habitual solitude. The Lord wants you to be free to enjoy sweet fellowship. If you struggle in this area, ask the Holy Spirit to shine His light into your heart and show you the reason. He will reveal and He will heal.

Gory Stories

Back to our boots! The enemy hates it when we share the love of the Lord. Instead, the devil will try to suck us into spreading gossip. The English dictionary defines gossip as idle talk - especially about the personal or private affairs of others. Negative chatter about others is gossip, even if what we are saying is true. Testimony is when I share my glory story. Gossip is when I share your gory story!

The Bible is clear about the damage gossip can do. It is an effective weapon of the enemy to shatter trust. It can destroy reputations, friendships and even churches. Proverbs 16:28 says, "A troublemaker plants seeds of strife; gossip separates the best of friends." (NLT). Strife may sound harmless but it is dangerous. Strife is when we are always rubbing one another up the wrong way. When strife creeps into life, frustration and irritation build and bickering becomes normal. Whilst love creates an atmosphere for encouragement, strife generates an environment for backbiting. Gossip opens the door for strife in every area of life.

Even talking about someone you dearly love can cause an irreparable rift. You might think that your motives for sharing were pure but there is always the chance that your intentions will be misunderstood. No one likes to hear that their personal issues have been discussed. The devil knows this so he tries to lure us into his hurtful habits. It is not only personal relationships that suffer. Gossip can hurt whole churches. Proverbs 26:20 says, "Where there is no wood, the fire goes out and where there is no talebearer, strife ceases." The devil desperately wants to get us telling tales because he knows they can run like wildfire through a whole congregation. Trust breaks down and believers get hurt.

The enemy always ensures his tricks are enticing. Proverbs 18:8 explains that "The words of a talebearer are like tasty trifles…" It feels good to our flesh to reveal a secret and it makes us powerful to be in the know. However, it harms us just as much as it hurts other people. The devil wants us to have our feet fitted with gossip, sharing things that aren't our business for all the wrong reasons. Why don't we kick off his footwear and leave his ugly ways behind us? Discretion is precious to the heart of God and it protects His people.

Take the Shield - Faith or Denial?

The purpose of a shield is to protect. When we hold the shield of faith, we are actively believing God's Word and refusing to listen to the devil's deceptions. When we hold onto the truth of God's Word, it protects us from the countless lies the enemy tries to tell. For example, satan will whisper: "You're not good enough", or "You'll never quit that habit", or "You're a disappointment". The devil may say it directly or he may use a man or a woman to lash out at you. Every hurtful, destructive word is an arrow which is intended to cause injury. When we hold the shield of faith, we are choosing to believe what God says instead. When we reject satan's accusations, we are extinguishing his fiery darts.

The devil has a cunning counterfeit. He tempts us to take up the shield of denial. God's Word comes to shine a light on the kinks in our character. The Holy Spirit often uses the people around us to point out our shortcomings. The Bible says that correction is one of God's tools for transforming and maturing His people. The enemy does not want you and I to receive correction so he offers us the shield of denial. When we hear feedback which highlights areas for improvement, we deny that we are missing the mark. We defend our actions and attitudes. We try to quash challenging comments.

Deflection

Sometimes we go a step further. We don't just deny, we deflect. We turn the conversation away from our issues and onto another person's errors. It is a way of avoiding having to face uncomfortable challenges. We take up the devil's shield to deny our shortcomings. The very word that would have set us free falls to the ground and dies.

The shield of denial has other uses too. It can be hard when God shines His light into our hearts to highlight hurt which is buried deep within. There will always be the temptation to pretend we feel no pain and gloss over it once more. God reveals something and then we must feel it so that He can heal. The devil wants us to refuse to make contact with old emotions for fear of losing control or facing past agonies. Denial stunts growth and keeps us bound by our history.

The Drummer Boy

Patrick and his sisters lived under a constant cloud of intimidation. Patrick's dream as a boy was to be a drummer. When his parents bought him a toy drum for his birthday, he was overjoyed. He sat on the stairs and played it non-stop. But the noise drove his father crazy. Just three days after Patrick received the gift, his dad snatched it, smashed it and hurled it out of the house. On several occasions, Patrick was punched in the face and beaten until he was blue.

By the time Patrick got saved in his late teens, he had been broken by his father's rage. He had a radical salvation and was deeply influenced by God's love. He wept daily for the first six months of his salvation as the Lord restored his soul, but he was not yet *fully* healed. Buried pain caused him to lash out occasionally at those he loved. You see, if we don't deal with every source of sadness on the inside, all too often we find ourselves behaving just like those who hurt us the most.

One of the enemy's greatest deceptions is to convince us that we are sorted when we are only *partially* healed. Twice in the book of Jeremiah, the prophet speaks of the dangers of stopping when we have received only a measure of restoration. Patrick had enjoyed a great deal of ministry. However, he was not yet fully restored. With a strong healing anointing, God reached into the hidden places of Patrick's heart and finished the work that He had started many years earlier. What a joy it was to see such release and relief. Uncontrollable anger became a thing of the past and Patrick discovered a freedom he had never known before.

The Helmet - Salvation or Downfall

If you are a cyclist, you will know that your most important piece of equipment is your helmet. The purpose of headgear is to protect you from any kind of head injury. Even if they are not terminal, head injuries can be life-shattering. The head of a company is its chief executive. The boss determines the direction that their organization takes. Your head contains your mind, which processes your thoughts, your imagination and your reasoning. Your mental activity determines your decisions. Your mind is critical to your well-being.

Ephesians 6 instructs us to put on the helmet of salvation. Soterion is the Greek for salvation. It literally means defense. We defend ourselves against the attacks of the enemy by taking captive wrong thoughts. Proverbs 23:7 says, "As he thinks in his heart, so is he." Our thoughts affect our attitudes, our moods and our behavior. The Hebrew word for salvation is yesua. It essentially means well-being. We protect our inner well-being by watching what we allow ourselves to think. We cannot stop an idea entering our minds, but we can stop ourselves dwelling on it. Philippians 4:8 instructs us to meditate on that which is good, true, uplifting and praiseworthy. Apply God's headgear and it will save you from many difficulties and disappointments.

Heavy

The devil wants you to wear a very different hat. Because your thoughts affect your life, he tempts you to take on a negative mindset. The Bible says that believers get what they expect (Proverbs 23:18). As a result, the enemy wants pessimism to permeate your thinking. He wants you to expect disappointment so that he has a legal right to serve it up to you on a plate. The enemy wants to feed you with fear-filled thoughts so that you don't step out and instead stay small. He wants you to meditate on his words of doubt and dread so that you will be discouraged and worried.

One year, the Holy Spirit banned my husband from thinking any sad thoughts. Before this time, he would sometimes find his mind drifting off in unhelpful directions. Like a dog off the lead, his thoughts would lead him down dead-end paths. One melancholy thought would lead to another. Soon enough, he found himself feeling dejected for no apparent reason. Taking captive every sad thought closed a dark door. He lived happily - as they say - ever after.

Ephesians 6:17 tells us to "...take the helmet..." In other words, we have a choice about which hat to wear. You and I don't have to tolerate negative thought patterns. There is one caveat. If your thoughts are rooted in low self-esteem, you will need to stay on a healing journey until your view of yourself matches God's opinion. Even while you are being restored, you do not need to accept negativity. It is a fight to keep your thoughts in line with God's Word, but it is a battle we can win. When you notice yourself thinking a negative thought, stop. Capture the thought, throw it out and replace it with something that is good. Replace pessimism with thoughts that are lovely and worthy of praise.

Two Swords - God's Word or Wounding Words?

God's plan is that His Word will fill our mouths. We are made in His image. When I say what Scripture says, there is power in my words. The Word works and has the power within it to defeat every attack of the devil. If I am feeling low, I can declare that "The joy of the Lord is my strength" (Nehemiah 8:10). I can decide that I will "...rejoice in the Lord always" (Philippians 4:4). Great authority is released when we put His Word on our lips. Things change. Isaiah 49:2 says, "And He has made My mouth like a sharp sword..." Our tongues were designed to both destroy the works of the devil and to build God's kingdom and His people.

The devil has perverted the purpose of words. The sword of satan is wounding words. They come in many forms: cutting comments, false accusations, put-downs, cruel names. The list could go on. Proverbs 12:18 says, "There is one who speaks like the piercings of a sword." These words crush and condemn. They ruin relationships and break hearts. They dash dreams and dent self-esteem. They can cause deep wounds.

Breaking Bullying

Evelyn was bullied from the age of seven. She wasn't as academic as other children so she was regularly sent out of the class for extra help. Every time the tutor came to pick her up, Evelyn would be overcome with embarrassment. She had few friends. Although Evelyn grew up in a stable home, her mom had been raised in a very abusive environment. Hurt people inevitably hurt people so Evelyn's mom would often tear her to pieces with cutting remarks. She told her daughter that she was chubby, selfish and spoiled. She criticized everything her little girl did and said.

Something about the mix of bullying at school and rejection at home made Evelyn crave approval. She was desperate to be accepted by her peers and longed for affirmation from her mom. As a teenager, Evelyn's fear of man escalated. She couldn't sleep and would become physically sick. The bullying continued. Evelyn suffered in silence, pretending not to mind as cruel words wounded her.

Evelyn got saved at college, married the son of a pastor and became a successful school teacher. However, one thing still bound her. She continued to be preoccupied with people's opinions. She was terrified of upsetting her in-laws, who she loved very much. Evelyn even had a panic attack in the middle of church one day as she was about to sing in the worship team. Fear gripped her.

Lodged Deep Down

At Healed for Life, the harsh words that had been spoken to Evelyn during her childhood came flooding back. She had buried them so deeply that she had almost forgotten how much they had hurt her. She poured out her pain in the presence of God as He healed her heart and repaired her brokenness. Afterwards, Evelyn felt an extraordinary joy and freedom - like she was a little girl again!

"When I returned to work, my colleagues said I looked different and that my face glowed!" Evelyn explained: "When I see people that I once feared, I look at them with joy. Even the children seemed to notice the difference! The best of all is that my relationship with God is better than ever. I found a wonderful new intimacy with Him. It is amazingly liberating to have my eyes on Jesus and not on the people around me! I can honestly say that since God healed me, my life is filled with joy and happiness!"

If you have been crushed by cruel comments, God wants to heal your heart. If you know that words have wounded you, go back to the chapters where we deal with the effects and stay on your healing journey. Perhaps you were surrounded by negativity as you were growing up and you find yourself lashing out at others in the way you were once attacked. The Lord is able to break the cycle. Allow the Lord to restore your heart and remove every cruel comment from your soul. Ask Him to make you more like Jesus, in both word and deed. Just as we can choose our thoughts, it is ultimately up to us what words we allow out of our mouths.

Whose Clothes Are You Wearing?

Now that we have looked at satan's counterfeits, I encourage you to ask the Holy Spirit to reveal any unwanted clothes you are wearing. We can remove the enemy's gear and put on the armor of God instead. It will suit you a lot better!

Heavenly Father,

The Belt

I realize that I have been believing lies about myself and about others. I apologize from the depths of my heart. I ask You to forgive me for being afraid of the truth. In reality, the truth is a safe place because you are the God of truth. I remove every form of deception from around my waist. Instead, I choose to gird myself with truth, knowing that it will bring me great freedom.

My Vest

Lord God, I thank You that Your word says that I am the righteousness of God in Christ Jesus. I ask You to forgive me for the times when I have felt justified by my own actions. I am sorry for thinking that I could earn Your love. Thank You that there are no boundaries to Your forgiveness. I am sorry for the occasions when I have felt that Your blood could not wash me clean. What a lie! Please forgive me, Lord. I discard every type of self-righteousness. Instead, I put on the breastplate of Your righteousness. I stand righteous before You because of Your righteousness.

New Shoes

Father, please forgive me for the times that I have engaged in gossip. It is not my business to talk about the affairs of other people. It wounds them and it hurts me. I am so sorry, Lord. I kick off the devil's shoes and instead choose to put on my gospel boots. The only person I will rush to talk about is Jesus Christ. I am His ambassador and I count it a privilege.

Shield

Lord, I realize that I have often defended myself out of turn. Instead of allowing my shortcomings to be challenged, I have resisted the truth and engaged in denial. Instead of facing my errors, I have deflected attention from my mistakes to the issues of others. Forgive me, I pray, oh Lord. I want to

148

be transformed to be more like you so I lay down the shield of defense that withstands correction. Instead, I take up the shield of faith and I will use it to extinguish every fiery dart of the devil.

Hat

Heavenly Father, I am aware that I have entertained many negative thought patterns. I have allowed myself to be dragged down into pessimism. I have listened to the devil's words instead of Yours. Forgive me, I pray, oh Lord. I take off the enemy's hat and will take captive every thought that does not line up with Your Word. Instead, I take the helmet of salvation. I will defend my well-being by thinking those thoughts that agree with Scripture.

Sword

Lord God, I realize that at times my tongue has been a sword that has wounded others. I am so sorry. Please forgive me. I ask You to cleanse my mouth. I ask You to give me greater self-control and I also choose to use my will to watch my words. I lay down the sword of wounding words. Instead, I take up the sword of Scripture. I will speak Your Word over my life and over the lives of others.

Heavenly Father, I ask You to help me daily to be aware of whose clothes I am wearing so that I can take up the full armor of God.

I thank You for Your goodness and kindness.

In Jesus' name, I pray,

Amen.

Chapter 12
HAPPINESS

When I have had a long, hard day, there is nothing like coming home and unwinding in my husband's arms. Nestling my head on his shoulder, all the stress rolls away and the tension lifts. Even though nothing around me may have changed, everything feels better. It is like that with God. When the enemy has been firing arrows at me from every direction, I absolutely love to linger in the presence of the Lord. There is no atmosphere that feels so cleansing and pure. His joy energizes me and His peace calms me. His presence is so very precious. Hebrews 13:5b says, "I will never leave you nor forsake you." That is His promise and it is very reassuring. It means that wherever we go, He will be with us. That is different, however, to enjoying the atmosphere of heaven here on earth.

Many years ago, my husband and I were enjoying a vacation in America. We rented a recreational vehicle and toured the south eastern states. Paul and I were together most of the time, sleeping, eating and living out of our mobile home. A few days into the vacation, I felt dry spiritually. I commented to my husband that I had hardly prayed all holiday. "Have you?" I asked. "Of course!" was his response. "I am always fellowshipping with my Heavenly Father," he said. We rearranged our itinerary to make time for us both to be alone with the Lord, but I learned a vital lesson that day.

To me, prayer was the hour that I would set aside. I would go into my prayer closet, talk to God, read the Bible and enjoy being with

Him. Then I would leave my secret place and pay Him little or no attention until my next prayer time. That was my prayer life. Imagine what that is like to God. We come to our King, celebrate and love on Him and then get on with our day. He never leaves us. He follows us wherever we go. The Holy Spirit goes to work with you and into every meeting. He joins you for a coffee and comes with you to lunch. He accompanies you to your friend's for dinner and then returns with you back home. He is with you wherever you go. God is with me every moment of every day, but how much of my attention do I give Him? It would be like spending the whole day with a friend and ignoring them.

Coming Close

James 4:8 says, "Draw near to God and He will draw near to you." He is always with us, yet this verse proves that He is not always as close to us as He would like to be. You can be sitting on a train next to a stranger. You are beside them, but you are not aware of them. You are minding your own business. The Lord will draw near any time we want. All we need to do is draw near to Him. What an amazing promise. To feel His presence and experience His love in any situation, all you and I need to do is draw near.

My husband and I were on the same vacation, but having two very different experiences. Every time he was quiet, he was fellowshipping with the Holy Spirit. He was worshipping in his heart and meditating on the Word. I was just getting on with life. I was not drawing near. Paul was refreshed and fully alive on the inside. I was dry.

Heart Whispers

Today, most mornings, my first thought is, "I love you so much Lord." I am drawing near, so His presence comes close. When

I am washing, I am worshipping. As I am waking the children, I am thanking the Lord for His goodness. No wonder it is so easy to enjoy Him in my secret place and hear Him as I read the Word. We have already been fellowshipping! Even at the office, all it takes is a longing from within. As you reach out on the inside, He draws near. As you wait in line at the grocery store, whisper from your heart that you love Him. I want to encourage you to make your heart a mobile home for the presence of God. It is a great way to enjoy genuine happiness.

As well as deliberately leaning in to the Lord throughout the day, it is important to cultivate an inner life that attracts the Holy Spirit. There are certain heart attitudes that pull Him close while there are others that push Him away.

Grumbling

Although we do not live under the Old Covenant, the Old Testament can give us great insight into the heart of God: "Soon the people began to complain about their hardship, and the Lord heard everything they said. Then the Lord's anger blazed against them, and he sent a fire to rage among them, and he destroyed some of the people in the outskirts of the camp." Numbers 11:1 (NLT). The Israelites were not grumbling on the mountaintop. That would be very ungrateful. They were complaining about their hardships.

It cannot have been easy to walk through the wilderness in soaring temperatures without a permanent resting place. Young families, pregnant ladies, nursing mothers and very old people. They all had to walk, day after day. If you are anything like me, you probably enjoy a variety of food. They had to eat the same meals every day for years! Despite the difficulty of their circumstances, God saw their grumbling as an appalling display of ingratitude.

Thank God for the cross. We live in the era of God's mercy, which means nobody is going to die today for complaining! However, we can hear God's heart on the matter: it grieves Him when we grumble. Although He will never leave us, the Holy Spirit will be kept at bay by our murmuring. In truth, it hurts us too. When we whine, it saps our energy and weighs us down. Words either bring death or breathe life (Proverbs 18:21). Negativity paves the way for discontentment and discouragement. It not only brings us down but it affects the people around us too. No one really wants to be around a whiner.

A few years ago, I brought one of my leaders on a ministry trip. We stayed in various places as I was ministering in several different churches. Unfortunately, nothing seemed to be quite right for my travel companion. The first day, the breakfast was not up to scratch. That night, the air conditioning was not strong enough. When we went to the next hotel, it was too cold. It was exhausting to be with her! I remember coming to God in prayer and He challenged me. "Are you going to allow her constant complaints to wear you down or are you going to bring her up higher?" This woman loved God with all her heart so I knew that once she saw her shortcomings, she would deal with her heart. We had a chat about the antidote.

Gratitude

Most of us probably know Psalm 100:4, which says: "Enter into His gates with thanksgiving..." The gates leading to a building are usually situated on the boundary of its land. They represent the first threshold that you must cross in order to make your way inside. If you cannot get through the gates, you will not be able to enter the building. In other words, an attitude of gratitude is essential to entering and remaining in the presence of God. The Message puts that verse like this: "Enter with the password: thank you."

Every time I choose gratitude, I am drawing near. Every time I say, "Thank you Lord for my job, my life, my family," I am releasing an irresistible invitation to the Holy Spirit to hover around my heart. It is not just something we say when something special happens. It is a constant expression from deep down. Thankfulness keeps our spirit light even when everything around us is dark. Gratitude generates joy which keeps us strong when times are tough. It has nothing to do with our circumstances and everything to do with our choices.

My Turning Point

A few years ago, in the middle of winter, I travelled to Pittsburgh to assist Prophet Cathy Lechner at a conference. I started to feel ill towards the end of it. Soon, I had a high fever. I carried on as best I could and faithfully attended every meeting. However, I was very glad when it was time to head home. I waved Prophet Cathy off, then waited at Pittsburgh airport for my flight to New York. As I sat at the gate, thick fog descended and delays were announced. I had to reach New York in time to catch my connecting flight to London. As long as the flight was not held up by more than two hours and thirty minutes, I could still fly home that night.

My eyes were glued to the departures board as the delay increased. Thirty minutes became an hour. Two hours became three hours. Before I knew it, I had missed my flight to London. At that moment, something inside told me not to let anything but thankfulness out of my heart. When I finally touched down in New York, my London flight was just taking off - without me. I stood in line at around 11pm to arrange a new flight home the following morning. By the time it was sorted, all the comfy seats in the cold, unwelcoming waiting area were gone.

A Long Night

I lined up four wooden chairs so that I could lie down. I put my purse under my head and pulled my coat over myself. Remember, it was February and the temperature inside was not much different from the freezing one outside. As I lay awake all night long fighting a fever, the only thing that left my heart was worship. I kept telling God how grateful I was for His goodness. I dwelt on the privilege of being able to call myself a minister. I told the Lord how much I loved Him over and over again.

When I eventually reached London, I waited at the carousel for my luggage. You guessed it: my bag did not arrive. I filled out the forms, then headed home - still loving on the Lord. Not one complaint arose in my heart during that 24 hour journey back to Britain.

The Heavenly Perspective

About two days later, my suitcase was delivered to my house. With a big smile, I thanked the delivery man and then my Heavenly Father. Just at that moment, I heard the Holy Spirit say: "Test passed." I was stunned. I had no idea I was sitting an exam! Not only that, His words meant the world to me. I had pleased my Heavenly Father.

As I look back, I believe that journey was my stepping stone to the next level of ministry. I also learned a lifelong lesson that night. God values gratitude. The best route through the toughest of times is thankfulness. Remain appreciative in the midst of the fire and you will have a good chance of remaining joyful. Not only that, the Lord responds to it with the highest prize of all: His wonderful presence.

Research Confirms God's Word (Of Course!)

I did a little research recently that blew me away. Not only does a thankful heart attract the Holy Spirit, multiple studies show that it improves our quality of life. There is a strong link between gratitude and general well-being. Let me mention just a few of the benefits:

- Gratitude increases happiness;
- Thankfulness reduces depression;
- Grateful people sleep better;
- Those who are thankful have higher self-esteem;
- Appreciative folk find it easier to build relationships;
- Having a thankful heart increases mental strength;
- Gratitude even improves physical health.

You must remember that for the research to be valid, they had to compare people facing similar circumstances. The differentiator was how thankful the subjects were, despite their surroundings. We can always decide to be grateful.

Choosing To Remember

We all know people who have it all (or nearly) and yet seem dissatisfied. On the other hand, it is humbling to meet those who are always overflowing with joy despite life's difficulties. After God delivered the children of Israel from the Egyptians, He instructed them to instigate an annual feast. And what was the purpose of this party? "This annual festival will be a visible sign to you, like a mark branded on your hand or your forehead. Let the festival remind you always to recite... "With a strong hand, the Lord delivered you from Egypt." Ex 13:9. God established an annual convention for one reason alone: so that His people would never forget His goodness. It was so important that they remembered God's goodness that He created a public holiday.

So how does that apply to you and I? How many times do we pray for something to happen, or not to happen? When God comes through, we may say thank you but soon forget His kindness. When we turn a corner and times are tough again, we quickly complain. The Lord wants us to make every effort to remember His goodness. When you face a trial, think back to your last testimony. When life is tough, remind yourself that God is good. Remember, gratitude cultivates the presence of God. You will be amazed how much happier life is when you practice pulling Him close.

The Dangers Of Strife

We have looked at the power of grumbling versus gratitude to repel or attract God's presence. I want to share a second set of opposing attitudes that either encourage or discourage the manifest presence of the Lord. Galatians 5:16 in the Amplified says: "Walk and live [habitually] in the [Holy] Spirit [responsive to and controlled and guided by the Spirit]..." This scripture speaks of a wonderful intimacy with the Lord where we can enjoy His closeness. The next verse goes on to explain that we must deliberately work to protect God's presence in our lives and reveals the attitudes that push Him away. The second half of verse 20 in the Amplified says: "...strife, jealousy, anger (ill temper), selfishness, divisions (dissensions)..."

Strife is one of the biggest peace killers known to man. It pushes God's presence away and produces discord and conflict. It is the tension that rises on the inside and causes us to quarrel and bicker. We feel frustrated and antagonistic. Sadly, it causes the Holy Spirit to pull back.

Terrible Twins

James 3:16 in the Amplified says: "For wherever there is... contention (rivalry and selfish ambition), there will also be confusion (unrest, disharmony, rebellion) and all sorts of evil and vile practices." Contention and strife are twins. The definition of contention is striving in rivalry. Contention is when we make life a contest. It is when we constantly compare our lot with the lives of others. It festers when we want to be right or recognized. According to the verse above, it only ever brings confusion and eventually opens the door to all sorts of problems.

A couple of months ago, we were getting ready to go out. It seemed that anyone who could let us down had done so that evening. I was frustrated and started to snap at everyone. My husband turned to me and corrected me sternly: "Do not bring strife into this house!" I immediately realized what I was doing and stopped. I apologized and calmed down. Strife never improves a situation. In fact, it always makes things worse. Our enemy is not flesh and blood, but the sooner we realize that strife IS our enemy, the better. So what is the opposite attitude that protects our peace?

What Would It Take For You To Be Content?

Contentment is powerful. Paul the Apostle explained that he had learned the secret of being content in every situation: "...I have learned how to be content (satisfied to the point where I am not disturbed or disquieted) in whatever state I am." (Philippians 4:11 Amplified). Notice that he said it was a lesson that he had to learn. It did not come automatically or without effort. Paul suffered terribly. He was beaten and shipwrecked. He knew what it was to be hungry and hated. Yet in all these things, he learned to be content.

Recently, I read a verse I know very well. I looked at it with a fresh perspective and it cut me to the heart. It was Hebrews 13:5: "Be content with such things as you have. For He Himself has said, 'I will never leave you nor forsake you.'" This scripture explains why we should be content. You and I should be satisfied simply because we have Him! You could put that verse differently: "Surely, I am enough for you?" In other words, when we are discontented, in our hearts we are saying: "Lord, You are not enough for me." Contentment is an expression of our gratitude to God for His presence. He is our reward, our joy, our life.

You are probably not contending with the persecutions that faced Apostle Paul. However, like Paul, we can choose to be content in any and every situation. We can simply maintain our peace, no matter what happens, and smile on the inside.

When we decide to stand back from the fray and replace contention with contentment, peace reigns. James 3:17 shows us alternative attitudes to strife: "But the wisdom from above is first of all pure. It is also peace loving, gentle at all times, and willing to yield to others. It is full of mercy and good deeds." Strife seeks to promote self. Consideration looks out for others. When we choose to put the feelings and needs of others above our own, strife drains out of our life. We are no longer battling or quarreling. Instead, we show graciousness and kindness. At the same time, it protects the presence of God.

I believe that as you start to practice these principles, it will lead you to a contented life. There is one more key to happiness that I would like to cover before we come to a close in prayer.

Mastering Your Emotions

There was a time when I had little control over my emotions. In fact, I think it would be fair to say that my moods ruled me. When all was well, I was full of smiles and pleasant to be around. However, when disappointments came along or life was tough, I was sullen. If my husband challenged me, I would feel hurt and I'd cry. If a friend misunderstood me, my stomach would tie itself up in a knot. Then there was my time of the month... I'd be irritable, weepy and gloomy. It was horrible.

It is not God's plan for you or I to be governed by our moods. If our feelings run our lives, then all it takes is some bad news or a cruel comment to ruin the day. That is not happiness! A friend spent some time working in another country. He explained how he felt angry all the time. "Everyone drives as though they are in a getaway car: spinning wheels, screeching brakes and cutting across lanes. I was furious by the time I reached the office every morning. I hated the place!" His emotions dictated the tone of every day. As a result, he was permanently stressed.

Out of Control

Proverbs 25:28 says, "Whoever has no rule over his own spirit is like a city broken down, without walls." Walls protect a city from enemy attack. So when our emotions are out of control, we are an easy target. We snap at the children or sulk in front of our spouse. We get upset with a friend for letting us down. We don't pray because we are in a huff. We won't go to church because we are too upset (and we use the excuse that it would be hypocritical when actually it would be helpful). The children staining the carpet or writing on the wall can rob us of our joy and even spoil our whole week.

Before my healing journey, if I was feeling insecure in the middle of the night, I used to wake my husband as he was drifting off to sleep. "Paul," I would whimper pathetically. "Do you still love me?" Can you imagine it? The guy is about to slumber and my insecurity jolts him awake! Feelings, feelings, feelings. To live in joy and victory, we need to master our emotions. In fact, Proverbs says we need to *rule* our spirits.

There is no doubt that this is easier to do when your heart is healed. However, just as you can be good with money whether you have loads of it or a little, so you can be in charge of your feelings whether you are hurting or whole. If you know you need emotional healing, book a space at Healed for Life and keep going until you know you are whole. God will lead you on a wonderful journey to stability and security. In the meantime, He will show you how you can take control.

Growing Up

As my love for the Lord grew, I wanted to be transformed to be more like Christ. I knew that to fulfill my purpose, I needed to be more mature. However, I did not like it when anyone told me what needed to change! It hurt my feelings. Eventually, I realized that if I wanted to grow, I would have to accept feedback. This became a training ground for managing my emotions. Instead of getting upset when people pointed out my shortcomings, I learned to bite my lip and listen. God used my desire to be mature to teach me how to take charge of my soul.

Many times women tell their husbands, "You never talk to me about how you are *really* feeling!" That was my mantra until the day my husband retorted, "Of course I don't! Anytime I try to tell you how I feel, you get upset and defensive." I apologized. The next time my husband attempted to discuss an issue, I remembered what he had said. I swallowed hard to push my tears away, bit my lip and listened. It was a turning point in my life. You might not get tearful when someone spotlights your shortcomings. Maybe you get irritated or angry. Whatever your reaction, handling feedback from your nearest and dearest is one of the best training grounds for managing your emotions.

Weaning Time

David described the experience of mastering his emotions in Psalm 131:2 like this: "Surely I have calmed and quieted my soul, like a weaned child with his mother; like a weaned child is my soul within me." The same strong leader who knew how to pour out his pain in God's presence also knew when to reel in his futile feelings. David likens the process of growing up emotionally to weaning a baby off milk and onto solids. Sometimes we see our souls as somehow untamable. However, the Bible likens our souls to a child that must be trained. This is profound. We need to see our feelings, thoughts and choices like a little one that needs to be matured. If I allow my soul to remain childish, I will never grow into full maturity.

The Bible says, "A fool vents all his feelings but a wise man holds back." (Proverbs 29:11). This is not a recommendation that we avoid pouring out our pain. Giving God our sadness is the healthy way to handle deep hurts. Venting is different. When we let it all hang out, when we let every issue spill over, we are falling short of God's best for us. To hold means to constrain, calm or quieten. Sometimes we must control our feelings. If we are upset with the way someone has spoken to us, we may need to swallow hard and get over it. On other occasions, we need to calm down. If we are angry or frustrated, we might need to speak peace to the storm inside. If we are irritated at the manner in which someone has spoken to us, we may need to take a deep breath, let it go and let them off. It is stressful and saps our strength when we give in to every whim.

If there are specific emotions that you often struggle with, such as upset or anger, search the Scriptures for verses that you can use to help pull you through. When you want to let things out, confess His Word over your life instead. Remember that you won't master things overnight. It takes weeks or months to wean a child and it takes time to wean our souls too. Nonetheless, if you ask daily for the help of the Holy Spirit, you will get there in the end. As you start to rule your own spirit, you will become a much better and happier you.

But Don't Massacre Your Emotions...

We are supposed to grow up emotionally, which means learning to control our feelings. However, that is not the same as shutting down. In His perfect maturity, our Heavenly Father is both expressive and constrained. He freely releases His feelings and yet knows when to hold back. As Christians, we can become experts at subduing our souls. Everything on the inside could be cooking and bubbling, but rather than releasing the pressures in prayer, we put a lid on it. We think expressing ourselves will somehow compromise our faith. We think that we will somehow be allowing in negativity. We need to learn to discern the difference between emotions that need to be expressed in prayer and feelings that need to be ignored. This creates great maturity. As a plant needs the right environment to grow, so faith thrives in a healthy heart. There are times for healing and there are times for just declaring that we are strong, even when we feel weak. That is why the Bible says: "Let the weak say I am strong!"

My Emotional Manual at the back of this book is a resource to help you. It covers most common feelings and provides you with a step-by-step guide to dealing with them in a healthy way. You can keep this book on your night stand and refer to it whenever you need help. It is possible to live a life of joy, security and peace. Learning how to handle your differing emotions is pivotal. As we close, let us go back to the beginning of this chapter.

Gratitude and contentment are two of the most powerful principles for living a full life. If you can combine them with growing in emotional maturity, you will be happy and unstoppable.

Heavenly Father,

I am so sorry for complaining. I realize my error and I choose to repent today. I want to get all negativity and ingratitude out of my life. Cleanse me, I pray. I also realize that I have allowed strife into my life. I easily become irritated and frustrated. I allow all sorts of silly things to wind me up and to bother me. Forgive me, oh Lord.

Today I choose to live a life of thankfulness. (Now spend two or three minutes telling the Lord all the things that you are grateful for). Help me to be grateful, no matter what is going on around me. Lord, You are enough for me. Help me to learn to be content. Help me to refuse strife and instead to allow gladness to arise within.

I love You with all my heart and I am so grateful for all You have done and continue to do for me.

In Jesus' name, I pray,

Amen.

MY EMOTIONAL MANUAL

An A-Z of How to Deal with Difficult Feelings

AFRAID

You may have a knot in your stomach or a terrible churning on the inside. Even thinking about the giant you have to face might make you recoil. Perhaps you are afraid of a person and the trouble they could cause. Maybe you are about to take a test or go for an interview. You might be terrified of making a mess. I think fear is one of our fiercest foes. It is amazing how often we tolerate it. I have heard otherwise strong people talk about fear of heights, spiders, rats, public speaking, driving in cities, driving on highways, and so on. The truth is that fear is a villain that seeks to control and torment its victims. I encourage you to see all angst as an enemy and to seek to overcome it in every area.

When God delivered me from fear, I realized that I was still afraid of one thing: horses. I like to go for long runs in the countryside and the route I usually took had a new set of visitors – some huge four-legged friends! For a few days, I avoided the offending field. It was easy to argue quite reasonably about this one: horses are much bigger than me and I am sure there must be stories of gruesome deaths by trampling! Let me stop there. Although we may be able to justify our jitters, remember that fear is not rooted in reason. You cannot convince someone who is terrified of dogs that your hound is friendly. Fear does not listen to logic. Any number of arguments about the affable nature of horses would not have quelled my anxiety. Reason will not defeat your fears either.

Make A Stand

One day when I was out running, I thought to myself, "Why am I tolerating any terror?" I had made a stand against fear and I did not want it to occupy any area of my life. Fear is believing the devil's threats rather than trusting God. It is sin. As I jumped over a small wall and into the field full of horses, I repented for being afraid. I declared, "Spirit of fear, I rebuke you in Jesus' name!" and I ran past the horses. I got through the field and rejoiced in my new victory. Now I had to go back the same way to return home! As I did so, there was a new peace. I said, "Jesus, I am safe because you are my shield." I ran through that field again and for the first time in my adult life, I had no fear of horses. All I had to do was repent of my sin, take up my authority in Christ and resist. I encourage you to do the same. The freedom you will enjoy in the end will be well worth the fight!

The Amplified version of 2 Timothy 1:7 says: "For God did not give us a spirit of timidity (of cowardice, of craven and cringing and fawning fear) but (He has given us a spirit) of power and of love and of a calm and well-balanced mind and discipline and self-control." Why do you think God tells us that, instead of fear, He has given us power, love and sound thinking? Fear robs us of all three!

Power

If you don't deal with fear, it renders you powerless to obey God, powerless to stand up for what you believe, powerless to honor God and powerless to say and do the right thing. When you are free from fear, you are empowered to make the right choices and obey God.

Love

When fear dominates, love cannot have its way in your life. If you are worried about what someone thinks, you might not contradict their opinion in order to support someone who is weaker. When you are afraid of people, you cannot be patient or kind. You end up being compelled to alleviate the intimidation. "He who fears has not been made perfect in love." (1 John 4:18b). When you are free from fear, love can flow through you to others and bring them joy and healing.

Sound Thinking

When you are gripped with dread, it clouds your judgment and overrides sensible decision-making. You lose your peace and you cannot think logically. When you are free from fear, you are able to judge what is best. You can make courageous and righteous decisions.

If you are ready to face and defeat your fears, there are two simple steps:

1. **Repent** - Tell the Lord that you are sorry for listening to the devil's lies rather than His word. Apologize for allowing fear to grip your heart. Repent for believing the enemy's threats instead of trusting in God.

2. **Resist** - As we know from 2 Timothy 1:7, fear is a spirit. James 4:7 tells us that when we resist the devil, he will flee. So after you have said sorry to God, take authority over the enemy. Just like I did, declare out loud, "In the name of Jesus, I take authority over the spirit of fear. You will no longer torment me. I bind you in Jesus' name and I drive you out of my life."

You will be amazed at the joy and freedom that come when you refuse all fear.

ANGRY

We all express anger in different ways. Some of us internalize rage and retreat. You may shut the door and allow your thoughts to fester. You don't let anyone in. Others of us become impatient, agitated and snappy. You could bark at people around you and make sure everyone knows you are cross. Some of us are huffy or moody. Maybe you are one of those who explode when anger reaches a crescendo.

If anger has built up inside you like a trapped whirlwind, it is important that it is released. You don't let this out in front of other people, but in prayer. If you feel incensed, it is vital that you release your steam in God's presence. Tell the Lord what has made you angry. David said: "I pour out my complaint before Him; I declare before Him my trouble." (Psalm 142:2). The Psalmist went to God and told Him exactly what had angered him, knowing that the Lord was the ultimate judge who could bring justice. Once you have told Him, leave every ounce of anger at His feet.

If you regularly struggle with rage, James 1:19-20 in the Amplified gives us some helpful pointers: "Let every man be quick to hear [a ready listener], slow to speak, slow to take offence and to get angry. For man's anger does not promote the righteousness God [wishes and requires]." Here is a step-by-step guide to dealing with anger towards the people around you.

1. Listen - It is amazing how much we all love to be heard. In contrast, the Bible tells us to listen to other people. We need to do this as carefully when we don't want to hear what they have to say as when we do. Simply taking the time to listen and making a point of trying to understand what others are saying will help a great deal.

2. Don't Speak - When we are angry, we are normally full of talk. Whether it comes out of my mouth or stays locked up within is not that relevant. If you can learn to slow down the inner argument it will help. The Bible says that love believes the best. It does not jump to conclusions, but is patient and kind. Let's refuse the rant that is trying to break forth and allow our hearts the chance to choose love. See that brother or sister as a child of God who therefore deserves your kindness.

3. Don't Take Offence - We like to use all sorts of words to disguise offence: "I'm not offended, I'm just cross...I'm not angry, I'm just upset!" These are simply different words for the same heart issue. If we hold onto any one of these negative attitudes for any length of time, offence will take root in our hearts. Once offence finds a home in us, it clouds our judgement, poisons our hearts and steals our joy. Offence is a choice, so refuse it every time.

4. Let It Go - Anger is not passive. It always creates negative energy on the inside and spoils lives. The final step is to let it go. God lets you and I off every time we miss the target. Let's be like Him. Let it go and keep letting it go until anger has no hold.

ANXIOUS

Worry is horrible. It eats us up on the inside, robs our peace and disturbs our sleep. It steals our joy and wears down our strength. Philippians 4:6 in the Amplified says, "Do not fret or have any anxiety about anything..." There is nothing that you are facing that warrants your worry. The currency of heaven is faith. We got saved by faith, we get healed by faith, we receive provision by faith and we must pray in faith. The way we access God's blessings is by believing His Word. I don't know what struggles you are facing. However, I do know that there is *nothing* too difficult for the Lord.

If we really understood our Heavenly Father's love for us and His concern for every aspect of our lives, our perspective would change. He cares about every issue that we face and has the power to make a difference. For us to receive His answers, we need to follow His instructions. The Lord does not ask us to ignore angst. He commands us to get rid of it. 1 Peter 5:7 in the Amplified says, "Casting the whole of your care [all your anxieties, all your worries, all your concerns, once and for all] on Him, for He cares for you affectionately and cares about you watchfully."

Enemy of Faith

We cannot muster faith when we are full of fear. We need to deal with anxiety so that we can put our trust in Him. The verse above tells us to cast all our concerns onto Him because He cares for us.

If we cast a stone, we throw it away. God wants us to hurl all our apprehension onto Him. When we hold onto an issue, it is up to us to sort it out. When we give it to Jesus, it becomes His problem.

When I was learning to live without worry, I developed a daily 'care-casting' habit. I would quieten myself in God's presence. Then I would name every single issue that was concerning me. One by one, I would tell God why I was worried and then cast each care onto the Lord. I would see myself throwing each problem into God's hands. The load would lighten. Then as I prayed, it would lift entirely. By the end of my session, I would be relieved and refreshed. I encourage you to do the same. Give God every angst, explain why you are worried and then deliberately give it to Him in prayer. Let go because God can change things whereas you cannot.

Get Some Rest!

Anxiety is exhausting. When we give Jesus our issues, He gives us rest. When we trust Him instead of worrying, He refreshes our souls. He pours out His Spirit afresh into our hearts and renews our vitality. "Come to Me, all you who labor and are heavy-laden and overburdened, and I will cause you to rest. [I will ease and relieve and refresh your souls.]" Matthew 11:28 (Amplified). The Lord does not want us to live with any anxiety. If you have gone from one concern to another, God wants you to change your lifestyle. You probably need to make care-casting a daily habit. Eventually, it will become second nature to resist angst. The Lord does not want us to accommodate any concern. Give it to Him today and then make a conscious decision to live without worry.

BETRAYED

Trust is the glue that holds relationships together. It builds a sense of safety and security. When I trust someone, I don't worry about what they will or won't say or do. I can relax in the knowledge that they are dependable. Trust creates confidence. When trust is broken, it can be devastating. It leaves us reeling with disappointment and feeling disillusioned. It can rock our view of families, whole sections of society and even churches. If one or two teachers mislead us, all too easily we mistrust educators in general. Likewise, if a church leader or pastor lets you down, you can end up being suspicious of all ministers. Betrayal is possibly the worst kind of broken trust. It is when we are forsaken by someone in whom we really believed. It is a violation of confidence and often involves unfaithfulness.

When we are betrayed, utter disbelief shatters something on the inside. It makes us want to retreat and build walls to protect ourselves. It changes our view of people and the world around us. Many years ago, some leaders we trusted nearly split our church. My husband Paul and I were devastated. As the dust settled weeks later, Paul asked me how I was. I clearly remember my reply: "I feel like I have been marched to the front of our church, stripped of my dignity and paraded on the platform in front of the people." That's what betrayal can feel like.

It Is Inevitable

The uncomfortable truth is that we will all experience betrayal's pain at some point or other. In fact, Jesus warned that it is inevitable: "Now brother will betray brother... and a father his child; and children will rise up against parents..." Mark 13:12. I don't know what you have gone through or who has let you down. I do know that you have probably experienced broken trust many times in your lifetime. It may have affected the way you relate to people. The enemy wants us to become guarded and wary as a result of life's difficulties. God wants us to grow to be more like Him. So how can we come out the other side better and not bitter?

1. Pour out the pain - Betrayal hurts. That is why we need the Healer. We need to go to God with our hurts as soon as they happen. After I shared my pain with my husband, I got into the presence of the Lord and told Him that I was deeply wounded. I told Him that I was shocked and disappointed and I cried in His presence. He released His healing love. I left my prayer closet refreshed. The road ahead was not easy, but I was ready to serve again.

2. Trust again - In the Psalms, we see David repeatedly declaring to the Lord, "I put my trust in You." When folk abandoned him and his co-leaders let him down, he got his heart healed and then chose to trust again. Trust is a choice. We must learn from the past, but it is better to become wise than wary. Once your heart is healed, I encourage you to declare, "Lord, I put my trust in You!" When we trust God, we can trust others - safe in the knowledge that our lives are in His hands. Even if we are hurt again, we can go to God and be healed.

COMPARING YOURSELF

Recently, I was flicking through Facebook when I saw a photo of a friend. She was pictured doing exactly what I had been believing God for years to achieve. Although I was genuinely delighted for her, I felt deeply discouraged. It made me feel like a fool: "I bet she never cut out pictures and put them in her dream book!" (Yes, that's right, I did and I have the book to prove it!). Her success made me doubt myself. I wondered why I was always falling short of my hopes and expectations. I got into the presence of God and started to pray, telling the Lord how I felt.

The Spin Doctor

Almost immediately, I felt a check in my spirit: I was listening to the lies of the spin doctor. The devil whispers untruths into our ears. He spins the stories of our circumstances to paint a gloomy picture. The Holy Spirit reminded me that God shows no partiality (Acts 10:34). What He does for one, He will gladly do for another. The very picture that God showed me to encourage me, the devil used to drag me down. As I sat in His presence, I apologized. I had allowed myself to be deceived by the devil and pulled into a state of discouragement. So I started to encourage myself in the Lord instead.

Do It Again!

I declared boldly, "Father, you are always faithful! Thank you for my sister's great success. I rejoice with her. I see it as a sign that my breakthrough is around the corner." In the Hebrew, the root meaning of the word testify is actually "do it again"! We are instructed to tell other people when God is good to us because it creates an atmosphere for more miracles. Every time a brother or sister shares their glory story, after we have celebrated their miracle, we can respond to God: "Do it again, Lord!"

Faithful Father

I do not know how long you have been waiting for God to fulfill His promises. Maybe things have happened around you that have discouraged you. Perhaps satan has been warping the story. Remember, although Abraham waited 25 years, he became the father of faith and had his son. Despite suffering terribly for 13 years, Joseph's dreams came to pass and he was promoted to the position of prime minister. Do not let the enemy tell tales about your circumstances. While you are praying and believing, God is at work behind the scenes to set the stage for your success.

DISAPPOINTED

Disappointment can pierce our souls. It can cause our hearts to sink and our spirits to stop soaring. When sadness comes, it sits like a heavy rock in our souls. It takes the wind out of our sails and usually sucks away our energy. All too often, our praise dries up and our prayer life feels muted. We might have suffered a series of losses and then one final disappointment becomes the straw that breaks the camel's back. Although it is something we frequently face, disappointment can be a real problem.

Despondent

I recently ministered to a young lady who was feeling dry and discouraged. She was born with a disease that affected her in a particularly personal way and she had been believing for her breakthrough for years. When we spoke, she had almost reached a point of disillusionment. After all, she had been persevering in prayer since her childhood, yet in the natural nothing had changed. Each day, she faced the same old struggles and she was worn out.

Her despondent eyes welled up with tears as she explained that the sense of sadness would come and go. Sometimes she was strong, but it didn't take much to knock her back. Church conferences could be confusing. Invariably, there would be prayer for the sick at some point. She wanted to believe, yet she was afraid of being let down. She responded to lots of altar calls with a guard around her heart. I asked her if she had ever told God how she really felt. She shook her head. I showed her how to pray in a way that would release the pent-up pain.

Being Real

Being real for the first time in a long time, this brave teenager opened up in prayer to God. She explained that she felt that He had let her down. She told her Heavenly Father that she was tired of fighting. This sweet young lady cried as she shared her bitter feelings and deepest thoughts. It is amazing the release we can experience when we express every sense of disappointment in His presence. One of the English dictionary definitions of intimacy is *'detailed knowledge or deep understanding'*. When we share our hearts with God in prayer, we are drawing near to Him. He always responds by drawing even nearer to us. The very process of pouring out our pain creates a new intimacy with the Lord.

After this young lady poured out her heart in prayer, she was visibly relieved. The disappointment which was covering her like a cloak lifted. Hope and faith started to fill her precious heart. She was ready to believe again.

Universal Problem

The thing about this issue is that it is universal. We all get disappointed. If we don't deal with it, each letdown will cause our heart to sink a little more. If it is left unchecked, a heaviness will settle within. This in turn can open the door to depression. (If disappointment has led you to depression, please read that chapter when you have finished this one).

If you have been surrounded by delays or felt weighed down by disappointment, it is time to lay it all down in God's presence.

When I tell people about my frustrations, I may feel a temporary release. When I pour them out before the Lord, it produces real relief. I once asked the Lord how we can really get rid of disappointment. I was amazed by what He revealed. As I have already shared, the first step is pouring out your pain in prayer. However, it does not stop there. He gave me a second important step.

The Offering

Once we have shared our hurts with the Lord, we need to give Him our disappointments as an offering. The thing about disappointment is that we feel entitled to be displeased. We believe we have been let down and deserve an answer. When we give up our right to be upset as a sacrificial offering, we can leave our prayer closet completely free. If this has spoken to your heart, why don't you take a moment to pray right now? God knows and cares about every inner struggle and He is ready to help you to become free.

DISCOURAGED

I do not know what you have been through, but I do know that discouragement is one of the devil's trusted weapons to take out God's people. There are many different words for discouragement in the Old and New Testaments. One word means to weaken, to slacken and to forsake (rapa). Another means to faint, to melt or to waste away (masas). A third means to cut down or shorten (qasar). These definitions lay out satan's plot for your life. The enemy wants you to throw in the towel. If he can't get you to give up altogether, he wants you to slow down.

Perhaps you were certain that you were about to get your breakthrough and then the cloud the size of a man's hand floated back out to sea. Maybe everyone around you has been getting blessed while you have waited on the sidelines for what feels like an eternity. It could be that you have been standing in faith, but you just don't know how much longer you will have to wait. Surely it should have happened by now? Perhaps people have made cruel comments that have caused you to crumple. Whatever caused it, remember that discouragement is dangerous and it seeks to delay or destroy your destiny. We need faith and focus to fulfill our purpose so we cannot tolerate it in our hearts. Let's look at three steps that will help us to kick discouragement out of our lives.

1. Remember Our Heroes Struggled Too

Abraham and Sarah were promised they would have a son, but nothing happened for more than two decades. Delay does not mean denial. 25 years later, they held their baby boy. King David was given a word when he was a teenager that he would rule over Israel. After a brief period of prominence, everything went horribly wrong and the young warrior spent ten years on the run. Then a week after his darkest day, David was made King of Judah. Joseph had a dream that he would be great, but he spent 13 years as a slave and in prison. Then one day, he was promoted straight from prisoner to prime minister. The God who has done it for them will also be faithful to you and me.

2. Remind yourself

Go back to the promises that God has given you. Dig out scriptures that confirm them. Remind yourself of every time that the Lord has come through. Shift your focus from your circumstances to His greatness. He is faithful and He is able.

3. Rebuke the devil

I started by saying that satan uses discouragement to derail God's people. It is time to defeat the devil and kick discouragement out of your life. Rise up on the inside and rebuke every doubt. Discouragement is when we lose courage. Joshua 1:9 says, "Have I not commanded you? Be strong and of good courage; do not be afraid, nor be dismayed, for the Lord your God is with you wherever you go." Take courage. The same God who did it for Abraham, Joseph and David will come through for you.

DEPRESSED

Do you feel a sadness beneath the surface that will not go away? Has the motivation to thrive wilted? Do you feel a dullness or a blankness inside your soul? Too many people suffer from depression and many others find themselves battling with some of the symptoms. Doctors define depression as periods when sad thoughts dominate. When we are battling with any form of depression - whether it is a full-blown clinical problem or a season of sadness - the temptation is to focus on ourselves. We tend to dwell on negative thoughts about our own lives.

If you are dealing with serious depression, you will almost certainly need healing and deliverance. Most major inner struggles are rooted in unhealed hurts and trauma. By God's grace, you are already experiencing healing through your reading, and He who begun a good work will be faithful to complete it. In the meantime, wherever you find yourself on the depression spectrum, there are two important biblical principles that can help us to find freedom:

1. Thoughts

Our thoughts influence our emotional state. The Bible says that "…as a man thinks in his heart, so is the man…" (Proverbs 23:7). This means that my musings affect my mood. You can test this out. At any given moment, stop and analyze your thoughts. Ask yourself if they are upbeat, downbeat or somewhere in between. Then evaluate your mood. You will realize how much your thinking affects your disposition.

Sad thoughts may seem innocent, but they can be dangerous. When there is pain buried inside, we need to pour it out. Sometimes sadness tries to burrow its way into our hearts by filling our minds with forlorn thoughts. The good news is that we can choose what we think. Of course our minds will drift in all sorts of directions, but we can decide to bring them back again. The Bible likens rogue thoughts to prisoners on the run: "Bringing every thought into captivity to the obedience of Christ." 2 Corinthians 10:5.

You don't have to dwell on all the ideas that drop into your head. You can arrest wrong thoughts and kick them out. Simply stop that train of thought, say no to yourself and turn your focus to something else. Philippians 4:8 says, "Finally, brethren, whatever things are true, whatever things are noble, whatever things are just, whatever things are pure, whatever things are lovely, whatever things are of good report, if there is any virtue and if there is anything praiseworthy—meditate on these things."

Slowly But Surely Spiraling

Recently, as I was on my way to minister in Florida, sadness tried to settle in my soul. My elderly father was fading away in a hospital thousands of miles away. I had prayed about whether to go on the trip and heard the Holy Spirit tell me to go. Knowing I was in the center of God's will did not diminish the sense of separation. The rest of the family was surrounding my dad with love while I was far away. My emotions were slowly spiraling. Suddenly, I became aware that I could choose my mood. Even in dark and desperate circumstances, we have a choice. I am not neglecting the importance of releasing pain. I am emphasizing that we can decide what we dwell on. Instead of focusing on my absence, I started to thank God that my father's life (and the day of his death) were in God's hands. I entrusted my dad into my Heavenly Father's everlasting arms once again.

Quickly, I took hold of my thoughts and brought them back to the task at hand. I resisted the spirit of heaviness and looked on God's goodness. I was on a mission and there were people's lives in the balance. Instead of sadness, I chose to thank the Lord for the privilege of ministry. I took my eyes off my own situation and reminded myself why I was alive. Joy started to stir again on the inside. Although it looked as though my dad had just a day or two left, the Lord kept him alive until I could return and say goodbye. I visited him in hospital before he slipped away peacefully into glory. I gave my grief to the Lord and He healed my heart. Heaviness knocked at the door of my heart, but it did not find a way inside.

It's Not Fair

Sad thoughts are not our only enemy when it comes to depression. Self-pity is often the sinking sand that sucks us down. If you feel like life is unfair, if you think that no one understands, if you believe that your burdens are too heavy or that you have it harder than most, you are probably contending with a foul opponent called self-pity. It is a dangerous destiny destroyer, but it can be defeated. If that sounds like you, go to the section on self-pity. Be sure to come straight back here when you are done.

2. Praise

There is a weapon available to us all that has power over depression. It is called praise. I am not speaking about lively songs at the start of your Sunday service. I am referring to something that comes from deep within - a choice to rejoice that utterly confounds the devil. I invite you to make a covenant of praise. You could decide to do this for a few days, a week or even a month. Pick a time of the day or night when you can be alone. I suggest you choose the hour when you are most likely to be at your worst. Set aside at least ten minutes to praise God with all your soul and strength. Isaiah 61:3 describes a divine exchange that happens when we exuberantly celebrate the goodness of God. The garment of praise literally expels the spirit of heaviness from our lives. If you treat praise like a daily medicine, you could experience deliverance from heaviness in just a few days.

The Midnight Hour

Rosa's husband Marcos died very suddenly after 30 years of marriage. Their two adult sons had already left home so this untimely separation left Rosa feeling desperately alone. After the funeral flowers had faded and everyone else had returned to normal life, Rosa found herself slipping into depression. Once a cheerful character, this dear lady was now somber and deflated. Nights were the hardest time as she lay awake with her memories. Rosa came to our ministry for help and God spoke to me very clearly, "Prescribe daily praise." I asked Rosa if she would faithfully take whatever scriptural medication I prescribed and she agreed. I shared what God showed me and I instructed her to praise Him through the midnight hour every day for a fortnight. Within a few days of high praise, the depression lifted. The garment of praise drove out the spirit of heaviness and Rosa was free. She then came to Healed for Life and poured out her pain in the presence of the Lord. The supernatural love of God filled her heart and she left completely healed and ready to live the rest of her life.

If They Can Do It, So Can We...

We read a terrible story in Acts 16. Paul and Silas brought freedom to a young girl who had been bound. However, instead of being thanked, they were accused of creating problems. Local leaders stirred up the magistrates against them. They were stripped and beaten with iron rods in the market square. It did not stop there. They were thrown into prison and then taken to the dungeon where their feet were fastened in iron stocks. It would have been dark, dirty and damp. Their backs would have been bleeding after their beatings and now their ankles were in fetters. What did Paul and Silas do? They gave God praise! While rejoicing, their chains fell off and the prison doors burst open. When we choose to celebrate His greatness in the midst of darkness, that same power is released from heaven to us free of charge.

EMBARRASSED

Recently, I was at a big conference with an array of amazing ministers. I spotted one of the main speakers who I had met two years earlier. As the gentleman walked past, I reached out to say hello, reminding him of our meeting. He glanced at me with what looked like a mixture of disgust and disbelief. He shrugged his shoulders and moved on. In a matter of seconds, I was cut down to size. I felt ashamed and embarrassed. King David spoke of the shame of being belittled. In Psalms 69:20 (Amplified), he said, "Insults and reproach have broken my heart; I am full of heaviness and I am distressingly sick..." Reproach is that unpleasant mix of undermining words and a dismissive or mocking attitude. With one cutting remark, we can be torn apart inside.

Put-downs

Perhaps you have been scorned by your partner, belittled by brothers, or insulted at the office. Maybe you were publicly humiliated. Whatever is said or done, it can leave us feeling stupid and small. Shame and dishonor can be excruciating. As a result, we often try to deny the way we are feeling. We think that if we ignore the inner churn, it will go away. We push it down, but we end up damaged by its effects. Even though my experience was relatively insignificant, it took the wind out of me. I regretted reaching out and wanted to withdraw. The enemy exploits this type of experience. He will tell us to avoid any behavior that could produce the same outcome. I was tempted to change my normally friendly outlook on life. This is one of the ways the enemy harms us in the long term. He causes us to step back, shut down and hide.

As soon as I felt these emotions rising within me, I pulled myself aside. I told God that this man's reaction had hurt me and I asked Him to heal my heart. It was not long before an inner peace was restored. I then let go of the offence. The following day when this minister was due to speak, my heart was open and I was expectant. I probably received more from his session than any other. The enemy's plan to rob my blessing had been thwarted.

The Way Out

If you have been embarrassed by the words or actions of another, God wants to heal your heart. If you have been disgraced, the Lord wants to restore your dignity. The first step is to acknowledge how uncomfortable the experience made you feel. Tell the Holy Spirit what you went through. Explain if you were squashed or humiliated. Be as real and specific as possible. Then ask your Heavenly Father to heal your heart.

The second step is to let go of the offence. The enemy wants you to hold resentment, but the Bible tells us that it is destructive. Forgive the person who humiliated you. Give them to God and let go of what they did. We never know why people do what they do so we cannot judge their actions. Give the incident and the person to God in prayer. I recommend you seal your restoration by asking God to bless the person who hurt you.

GUILTY

If any memories (however well hidden) still make you feel bad, God wants to set you free. When you confess your sins to God in prayer, you are forgiven. That is the end of the matter as far as God is concerned. His will is that nothing from your past can condemn you. That way, satan and sin lose their power in your life. I was riddled with guilt after I rededicated my life to the Lord in my early twenties. I felt stained by my sin. I knew I was doing wrong when I messed around so I felt disqualified from God's full forgiveness. The Holy Spirit led me to meditate on Romans 6:6: "Knowing this, that our old man was crucified with Him, that the body of sin might be done away with, that we should no longer be slaves of sin."

I began to realize that it wasn't just my sin that Jesus had taken to the cross: Jo the sinner had been crucified with Christ. That woman no longer lived. The person who messed up had been put to death with Jesus. Not only had the sin been done away with, but the sinner had been dealt with too! The new me was raised with Christ, clean and forgiven. It is exactly the same for you. The new you is blameless before God because of Jesus. He wipes away the deliberate iniquities and mistakes of all who are truly sorry. The same blood that is powerful enough to save us is equally able to cleanse us from every error. His work is perfected in all who ask for forgiveness.

Price paid

Isaiah 53:5 explains that Jesus was wounded and crushed for our transgressions and iniquities. A transgression is when I go somewhere I should not go. It is when I do something I should not do. It is rebellion. Meanwhile, iniquities are warped and perverted deeds. They often lead to patterns of bad behavior. Jesus was punished and took the blame for every one of our mess-ups. In return, He wants you and I to rest in the knowledge that the price has been paid. 1 Corinthians 6:11 in the Amplified says: "But you were washed clean (purified by a complete atonement for sin and made free from the guilt of sin), and you were consecrated (set apart, hallowed), and you were justified [pronounced righteous, by trusting] in the name of the Lord Jesus." Once we have repented, we are washed completely clean. We don't even smell of sin.

It makes no difference what you have done. It might be an abortion, a bad relationship, an outburst or a lifetime of wrong living. Perhaps you regret the years that you have wasted, opportunities that you have missed or prayers that you have not prayed. The Lord died for every mistake you have ever made. Once you say you are sorry and turn aside from wrongdoing, the old passes away and all things become brand new. There is no room for shame or guilt. Before God, you and I are blameless. You have probably heard the explanation of what justification accomplishes in us. When you trust in the cleansing blood of Jesus to wash you clean, in God's eyes it is just as if you had never sinned. When we are forgiven by Jesus, He looks at us as though we had never messed up in the first place.

Free!

Psalm 130:3 in The Message says, "If you, God, kept records on wrongdoings, who would stand a chance?" None of us would stand a chance if God made us pay for our mistakes. Your faults are no different to mine. I am forgiven today for impatience or pride in the same way that I was forgiven many years ago for impurity. The Bible says that God separates you from your sin 'as far as the east is from the west' (Psalm 103:12). So after you ask God to forgive you, He removes your wrongdoing from you. It is no longer yours. It has gone.

Isaiah 53:5b says, "The chastisement for our peace was upon Him..." Chastisement means punishment. He was punished for your faults. He was scourged for your sin. So why flog yourself? He took the blame so that you could rise up righteous. He does not want you to feel bad about old errors. He wants you to enjoy being righteous in Christ. He longs for you to know the inner peace that an innocent man or woman freely enjoys.

HEAVY-HEARTED

Heaviness of heart is horrible. It may be brought on by bad news or unwanted bills. Sometimes it comes as a result of stress and strain. When we are weary or overwhelmed, we can feel like there is a weight in our souls. Whatever the cause, it is a sinking sadness. It is as if a blanket is covering your heart. You are weighed down and despondent. When we are heavy-hearted, we find ourselves thinking thoughts we would not otherwise consider. We might think: "This is too much", or: "I feel like giving up". Maybe we say to ourselves: "I've had enough of all this." In Psalm 119:28, King David said, "My soul melts from heaviness." When we contend with any heart condition, it is good to know what the enemy wants to achieve. This verse shows that the devil intends to use that weight on the inside to cause you to melt. He wants you to be weak and weary. Ultimately, he wants you to give up. As well as being a horrible experience, heaviness is dangerous.

Heaven's Prescription

What should we do about heaviness? Isaiah 61:1-3 is not only an outline of Jesus' job description. It is also a list of human problems accompanied by heaven's prescription. Let's have a look at some of this passage: "The Spirit of the Lord God is upon Me, because the Lord has anointed Me to preach good tidings to the poor; He has sent Me to heal the brokenhearted, to proclaim liberty to the captives, and the opening of the prison to those who are bound... To comfort all who mourn... The garment of praise for the spirit of heaviness..." (Isaiah 61:1-3)

The poor in spirit need to hear the gospel. That's heaven's prescription for non-Christians. The brokenhearted need healing, not liberty. Those who are bound need liberty. That's their prescription. They don't need healing. Those who are mourning need supernatural comfort. They don't need freedom! Are you following me so far? Now let's get to heaviness. Heaven's divine prescription for that heavy-heartedness is not healing. It is not even prayer. It is praise!

Recently, I was feeling very heavy. It had been an intense few weeks packed with family challenges as well as a full ministry schedule. I was weary. That opened the door for the spirit of heaviness and even thoughts of despondency. I prayed and worshipped, but nothing shifted. I even asked God to send someone to encourage me. I was fed up and (for a brief moment) felt like giving up. I cried out to God to help me. Almost immediately, I was taken straight to Isaiah 61 and I knew what I had to do. I did not feel like praising. The enemy makes sure that we don't want to praise because he knows it will set us free.

Hebrews calls it the sacrifice of praise! We don't praise because we feel like praising. We praise because it is the right thing to do. We praise because He is worthy. And we praise because it is heaven's prescription for heaviness! I was out shopping when God told me to praise. I did not care who was watching. I just started to praise: "There is no one like our God, I will praise Him, praise Him..." Within seconds – yes, just a matter of seconds - the heaviness that had been hanging around for several days lifted. If you're heavy-hearted, don't delay. Start to praise and continue to praise until every last weight has lifted. I suggest you make it your lifestyle. Any time the enemy tries to pull you down, push him away with joyful praise! The devil hates praise so he always flees.

JEALOUS

What's the point of serving if I never get promoted? What's wrong with me? Why do others get opportunities? Why has he got his breakthrough when he hardly ever comes to church? Why has she got her miracle when she barely knows the Word? What is the point of praying and fasting when I am never the one celebrating victory? It is not fair! These are the type of resentments we feel and painful questions we ask when we compare ourselves with others. The sad irony is that while we compare our walk with someone else's and wish we had what they have got, our breakthrough can be delayed.

The Spiritual Root

The tenth commandment warns us not to look over our shoulder and crave what God has done for someone else: "You shall not covet your neighbor's house, you shall not covet your neighbor's wife, nor his male servant, nor his female servant, nor his ox, nor his donkey, nor anything that is your neighbor's." Exodus 20:17. If we look at something that belongs to someone else and want it for ourselves, that is covetousness. If we want their position, their promotion, their blessing, their job, their success or their house, we are directly opposing the tenth commandment.

The Bible says that the law of love fulfills all the Old Covenant commandments. If I love my neighbor as much as I love myself, then I will be as happy when they do well as when I succeed. The more we bless people who have what we want, the more we will remove jealousy from our soul. Let us look at how to evict it from our everyday lives:

1. Recognise The Problem

Some 'sins' are harder to own up to than others. There is something about jealousy that does not sound good. Remember that it is a very basic human issue that most of us will have to deal with at some time or another. Truth and then confession is always the starting point. Tell the Lord that you have been jealous and ask Him to help you to become free. If you believe it is rooted in rejection or insecurity, ask Him to heal you deep down.

2. Kick It Out

God's Word says: "Do not let your heart envy..." (Proverbs 23:17). This verse reassures me that you and I can stop jealousy in its tracks. If a jealous thought comes as a seed, don't allow it to take root in your heart. Kick the thought out and replace it with a generous, loving prayer. If you feel a pang of envy, you don't have to act on it. Instead, say or do something to celebrate the person of whom you are jealous. "Make no provision for the flesh, to fulfill its lusts." Romans 13:14

3. Be Content

Paul the apostle said that he had learned to be content in every situation - whether he experienced lack or plenty, or whether he was up or down. Contentment is a sign of gratitude to God for what He has ALREADY done. Work at contentment in your life and make thanksgiving a daily exercise. "Let your conduct be without covetousness; be content with such things as you have." (Hebrews 13:5)

4. Bless

So how should we handle the blessing that God pours out on those around us? Rejoice with those who do better than you. Pray that those you compete with will be raised to greater heights and glory. That will soon knock jealousy on the head! Be generous with your prayers and desires. Put the goals and aspirations of others above your own destiny. It will help enormously.

LET DOWN

Did you feel certain that something special was about to materialize, but then nothing happened? Maybe you were believing that your breakthrough was imminent but the "cloud the size of a man's hand" drifted back out to sea. When we have been expecting a miracle but the opposite occurs, it can be awfully disheartening. Too many times to mention, I have been sure that my suddenly was upon me. I believed that I was about to see a turnaround in my circumstances, but then nothing changed. What do you do with those moments? How do you deal with the disappointment? How do you avoid being dragged into discouragement?

I love how honest the psalmists were with the Lord. They told Him exactly how they felt and then found their way back into faith. Asaph, who wrote 13 psalms, was one of David's worship leaders. He was close to the king and had a similar openness of heart in prayer to God. Around the time that Asaph wrote Psalm 77, he went through a terrible trial. He was deeply disappointed and felt let down by the Lord. But he dealt with his conflicting feelings. I believe this psalm was written to help us handle such seasons.

1. Let It Out

First, Asaph had it out with the Lord! He vented his frustrations to his Heavenly Father. He clearly felt terribly let down by God: "Will the Lord cast off forever? And will He be favorable no more? Has His mercy ceased forever? Has His promise failed forevermore? Has God forgotten to be gracious? Has He in anger shut up His tender mercies? And I said, 'This is my anguish...'" Psalms 77:7-10

He told the Lord exactly how he felt and vented every sense of injustice. He even asked God if He had forgotten His covenant. He poured out his deep disappointment. He said the things that you and I are often afraid to say. I believe these verses are in the Bible because God wants us to know that He can handle our frustration. If you are feeling let down, let the Lord know. Express your anguish or outrage. Vent your feelings in prayer. That is the right place for release. Be as honest as you can.

2. Pick Yourself Up

After Asaph had given all his grievances to God, he was ready to encourage himself again. "But I will remember the years of the right hand of the Most High. I will remember the works of the Lord; Surely I will remember Your wonders of old. I will also meditate on all Your work, And talk of Your deeds." Psalms 77:10b-12. He chose to remember God's goodness. I encourage you to join Asaph and focus afresh on the faithfulness of your Heavenly Father. Remember all the great things that He has done for you in the past. He never changes. What He has done before, He will do again.

By the time Asaph had finished thinking about the blessings of God, He was encouraged and was ready to believe again. He was rejoicing and his heart was happy: "Who is so great a God as our God?" Psalms 77:13b. There is great power in pouring out our pain. However, we can't stop there. Once we have told God how we feel, we must be quick to turn our hearts to praise. Hebrews 13:15 says, "Let us continually offer the sacrifice of praise to God..." Praise starts as a great sacrifice but soon becomes the place of our breakthrough.

LONELY

Being alone can produce a deafening silence. Walking through the door that was once shared with someone special. Sitting by yourself with a knot in your stomach. Loneliness can feel like a cold cloak separating you from companionship and love. It may be that you have people around you, but you still experience a deep, unmet need for friendship or love. Perhaps you are unable to share your thoughts and feelings freely.

Not What It Seems

A cold marriage can be a desolate place. People assume you have it all, yet you feel empty and alone. You long for intimacy, looking back at the times when you shared so much. You feel like you are just sharing a house together, or you're merely roommates. I remember being on my own at a conference in a foreign country. There were crowds in every direction, but I felt alone. At a lunch for special guests, ministers dined with their travel companions while I sat by myself at a table for two. No one did anything to wound me and yet I felt hurt by the isolation. I looked around pretending to be searching for someone when really I was looking for anyone. Loneliness can feel like rejection.

The Way Out

David felt that way at times: "Turn to me and be gracious to me, for I am lonely..." Psalm 25:16. He was crying out to God saying, "I feel isolated and it hurts!" On nearly every step of his journey,

King David was surrounded by people. Loneliness isn't always a lack of relationships. Loneliness is often an issue of the heart. It can be resolved in God's presence. It is amazing what happens when we openly share our loneliness with the Lord in prayer. As we pour out the pain, He will pour in His liquid love. Sometimes it is rooted in hidden sadness, so if you are struggling, allow the Lord to do a work from the inside out.

When I first started travelling to the US, I was worried about being alone. Ten hour flights followed by empty hotel rooms seemed isolating. I went to God in prayer. He revealed Himself to me as my closest companion. Now I love the time by myself. I do not feel alone. I feel loved. If you are lonely, I encourage you to be real with God in prayer. Tell Him how you are hurting and then ask Him to help you to feel His companionship. He will never leave you nor forsake you. He is always with you and He wants you to experience Him as your closest friend. Psalm 27:14 says: "He shall strengthen your heart". After you have opened up to Him about how you are feeling, ask Him to create an inner stability and strength.

The Lord wants us to enjoy friendships with our brothers and sisters as well. The best earthly relationships are born in heaven, so ask God to knit you together with the people who will help you to fulfill your purpose. He is faithful.

OVERWHELMED

Have you ever felt like everything is just too much? You may have been working tirelessly towards your goals with little or nothing to show for it while the mountain still to climb towers above you. Perhaps life has been hitting you with a different trial at every turn: family challenges, financial trouble, ministry problems, health worries. It goes on and on. King David used the term overwhelm. The dictionary definition is overpowered or overcome. When floodwaters overwhelm a village, they invade, they cover and they bring destruction.

It is dreadful to be overwhelmed. It makes us feel like quitting, like giving up on our goals and giving in to defeat. We reach the point when it seems as if it is all too much and we cannot carry on. We know that King David felt overwhelmed at times. That tells me that even the strongest of leaders contend with this issue. So what do we do about it? It is clear that we need to escape the torrent of discouragement that it brings - and we need to get out quickly.

As a year of hard work and challenges drew to a close, I found myself feeling downhearted. I was facing one thing after another. Before I knew it, my joy was waning and sadness inside was building. The problem was that I had a big event ahead of me and I could not afford to falter. I had been working harder than ever to see Healed for Life established and yet kept facing soul-destroying setbacks. Although we had made amazing progress, all I was aware of was the size of the assignment. I was discouraged, disheartened and disappointed. I went to the Lord in prayer and He showed me what to do. You may not be feeling it right now, but the chances are you will need this someday. Here are three steps to counteract being overwhelmed.

1. God is bigger

In Psalm 61:2, David prayed, "When my heart is overwhelmed, lead me to the Rock that is higher than I." We need to know that God is bigger than the things that are bigger than us. He can handle the things that are too great for us. He has got this, and He has got you. He is your Rock. That means He is stable, unwavering, immovable and safe. First of all, allow that truth to sink into your soul.

2. God won't fail

Second, bring your bewilderment to the Lord in prayer. Tell Him how you are feeling and ask for His help. When I did that, I was moved to tears by the words I heard: "I will not fail you." I want you to hear those words too. Your Lord, your Heavenly Father, will not fail you. His ways are not our ways (which can make life extra painful while we wait), but His promises are always yes and amen. Psalm 25:3 says, "No one who trusts in You shall ever be disgraced." Keep trusting. He will not let you down.

3. Give up!

Anytime our hearts and minds have been overwhelmed, we are clearly carrying a host of cares. 1Peter 5:7 in the Amplified says: "Casting the whole of your care [all your anxieties, all your worries, all your concerns, once and for all] on Him, for He cares for you affectionately and cares about you watchfully." It is time to give every concern, every angst, every worry and every fear to

God in prayer. See yourself giving over every issue to the Lord. When we hold onto a problem, we have to solve it. When we give it to God, He has to take care of it. I know whose hands I would rather trust!

SAD

Sometimes we feel sad, but we just don't know why. If that is you, it will be important to start by asking God to reveal the reason. We looked at Rebekah's Request in Chapter 2 of this book. Go back and read that section. Then go to God using her prayer and ask Him to show you why you are feeling so sad. He is faithful and He will shine His light on the source of your sadness. Once we know what we are dealing with, we can find relief and healing. Perhaps you have a heavy heart. Maybe the sadness in your soul is not the result of a specific hurt or pain. It could be that you are weighed down and feeling low. If that is you, please go to 'Heavy-hearted' earlier on in 'Your Emotional Manual'.

Sorrow

If you are still reading, I am assuming you know why you are sorrowful. If you are still unsure, God is faithful and He will lead you out anyway. Sadness slows us down and feels like a cloak over our souls. Maybe you have lost someone you love very much. You might have drifted apart or perhaps they passed away. It could be that they walked away. Maybe your hopes and dreams have been dashed. I want to encourage you to talk to the Lord about the source of your sadness. You may feel as though you have missed the mark and you are afraid that you may have derailed your destiny. Perhaps life took a turn for the worse and it seems like you have had to settle for second best.

Pour it out

Let me remind you what Lamentations 2:19 says: "Pour out your heart like water before the face of the Lord." More often than not, sadness must be expressed with both words and tears in prayer. When we put our pain into words, it gives voice to our sadness. It enables us to release the sorrow and find relief. Tell God what happened and explain exactly how it made you feel. Share your regrets and express your sense of loss in as much detail as possible. Words are like the cork in a bottle. The wine represents our pain. When we say what we never said, we remove the stopper and we can pour out our pain in His presence.

New hope

Once you have released your sadness, it will be important that you open your heart afresh to hope. There is no situation that God cannot turn around. There is no problem that He cannot solve. There is no pain that He cannot take away. Jeremiah 29:11 (NIV) says, "For I know the plans that I have for you, plans to prosper you and not to harm you, to give you a future and a hope." Notice the word does not say plan but plans. God does not have just one plan. He has many amazing plans. When things do not go the way we wanted, He restores us and then reroutes us onto a new path of blessing. Ask God for a fresh promise from His Word. He is able to take away all your sadness. He is also able to give you hope and the expectation of a good life ahead.

SELF-PITY

The Bible teaches that each one of us is unique. God has a tailored plan for your life that reflects your individual design. At the same time, one of the core lessons of Ecclesiastes is that nothing we go through is new: "That which has been is what will be, that which is done is what will be done, and there is nothing new under the sun. Is there anything of which it may be said, 'See, this is new'? It has already been in ancient times before us." (Ecclesiastes 1:9-10)

Survivor

In the years after our daughter died, I saw myself as a survivor. I was someone who had been to hell and back, and made it out alive. I believed that I deserved extra compassion because of the loss I had suffered. When times were tough, I expected special concessions. When life was good, I saw myself as a hero for being happy. Most of all, I saw myself as different. When we see ourselves as different, we make allowances for all sorts of things. We accept isolation, allow negative thinking and excuse bad behavior. When we believe our lives are unusual, we often think that we can't achieve the breakthroughs that others enjoy. Self-pity can leave us feeling cheated and dejected. It erodes our faith, makes us feel like downing tools and giving up. Left unchecked, self-pity is a destiny destroyer. It causes its victims to be preoccupied with themselves.

In truth, I was not that different from anyone else. History repeats itself. Countless couples across the world have lost their children to an untimely death. Indeed, many have lost entire families. Scores of parents have suffered like me and come out strong from the experience. In the same way, others have endured battles that are similar to yours and emerged successfully on the other side. Every test or trial has been faced by others down through the centuries (1 Corinthians 10:13). When we realize that our struggle is not all that different from the battles that others have had to fight, it can help us to put our lives in some sort of perspective. If we take our eyes off our individual issues and instead look to the greatness of God, the Lord can start to work within.

Sad End

I find the final scenes of Elijah's life sad. After one of the most extraordinary victories on Mount Carmel, defeating the prophets of Baal and proving the power of God, Elijah ran away, terrified of Jezebel. He escaped to a cave whilst displaying some telltale signs of self-pity. When we feel sorry for ourselves, we often want to retreat and hide somewhere where we can wallow in our circumstances. We believe the lie that our pain is unique or our circumstances are the worst. Elijah cried out to God that he was the only servant of His who was alive. Yet the Bible states that there were 7,000 men and women who maintained their faith in Yahweh. Believing that he alone was left, Elijah told the Lord that he wanted to die. Self-pity always tells us to give up. It was at this point in Elijah's life that God called time on this mighty man of God and raised up Elisha in his place.

If you have been feeling sorry for yourself, I encourage you to do two things. First of all, acknowledge deep down that you are not alone and that your troubles are common to man. Others have fought the battles you are fighting and come out as conquerors.

You can too. Second, allow gratitude to rise up on the inside. Think of every good thing that God has done for you over the years and start to thank Him from the bottom of your heart. Gratitude is the greatest antidote to self-pity.

WEARY

Recently, I found myself feeling really weary. I was left jaded by constant challenges coming from every direction. I was fed up of fighting. I was tired of having to push and press. It was one thing after another and I wanted a break. The thing is, doing the will of God does not usually drain us. Jesus said, "My burden is light, and my yoke is easy." Fulfilling our purpose is more likely to energize than exhaust. It is not getting the job done that wearies us, but the setbacks and hurts along the way.

Not Again!

I did not want to hear another "No" or "Not this time". I did not want to fight for every inch of advancement. Just once, I wanted to see miraculous breakthrough before I even asked. I wanted everything to work out and I wanted God's promises to fall into my lap. The Bible gives us two opposing instructions when it comes to weariness. That is why we need to understand exactly what is going on inside so that we can take the right scriptural medicine.

Get Refreshed

Matthew 11:28 says: "Come to me, all you who are weary and burdened, and I will give you rest. Take my yoke upon you and learn from me, for I am gentle and humble in heart, and you will find rest for your souls." When we are spent and flagging, Jesus says something like this, "Come and spend some time in My presence. Pour out your heart before me. Offload on Me and then

I will fill you up afresh." So, I did just that. I pulled myself aside and poured out my heart to Jesus. I told Him I was fed up of fighting and I was tired of testing times. I cried, then I sat in His presence and worshipped. He refreshed me and replenished my strength. Weariness washed away as He breathed new life into my heart. It did not stop there. My spirit was revived, but my mind still needed renewing.

Get Up!

The other New Testament instruction about tiredness is in Galatians 6:9: "And let us not grow weary while doing good, for in due season we shall reap if we do not lose heart." Here we are warned of the dangers of giving in to tiredness. We have to make a choice to get up and go again. We need to kick every trace of discouragement out of our life and remind ourselves once more of His promises. I got hold of God's Word again and spoke strength to myself: "Jo, you are well able, you were designed for this. Every purpose and plan God has for you shall stand!" This journey to fulfillment is a fight and it is a marathon. However, there are water holes for refreshment all the way there. If you are feeling dry or burned out, it is time to get revived in His presence. Then get back up and go again.

WHAT NEXT?

Your heart is probably your most valuable, and yet your most vulnerable, asset. This book is just part of your journey to wholeness and freedom. As you finish this book, make the decision to continue to prioritize your inner wellbeing. Refer to *My Emotional Manual* any time you are dealing with negative feelings. Visit our website JoNaughton.com. Sign up for our free weekly blog, get our books and find out about our events near you. Above all, look after your heart every day of your life for it determines the course of your life.

I am convinced and sure of this very thing, that He Who began a good work in you will continue until the day of Jesus Christ (right up to the time of His return), developing [that good work] and perfecting and bringing it to full completion in you. (Philippians 1:6 AMP)

Let the above word sink deep into you. God is preparing you for your destiny. He has already started the job, and He will be faithful to finish it.

An Invitation

If you would like to ask Jesus to become the Lord of your life, I would be honored to lead you in a simple prayer. The Bible says that God loves you and that Jesus wants to draw close to you: "Behold I stand at the door and knock. If anyone hears My voice and opens the door, I will come in." (Revelation 3:20). If you would like to know Jesus as your Friend, your Savior, and your Lord, the first step is to ask. Pray this prayer:

Dear Lord,

I know that You love me and have a wonderful plan for my life. I ask You to come into my heart today and be my Savior and Lord. Forgive me for all my sins I pray. Thank You that, because You died on the cross for me, I am forgiven of every wrong I have ever committed, and I am completely cleansed from my past. I give my life to You entirely and ask You to lead me in Your ways from now on. In Jesus's name, amen.

If you have prayed this prayer for the first time, it will be important to tell a Christian friend what you prayed, and to find a good church. Just as a newborn baby needs nourishment and care, so you (and all Christians) need the support of other believers as you start your new life as a follower of Jesus Christ.

At harvestchurch.org.uk, you can listen free to Bible messages that will help to build your faith. You can follow me on Twitter (@ naughtonjo), go on Facebook and like my public page (Jo Naughton) and follow me on Instagram (@naughtonjo). God bless you!

About the Author

Jo Naughton is the founder of Healed for Life, a ministry dedicated to helping people be free to fulfill their God-given purpose. Together with her husband, Paul, Jo pastors Harvest Church in London, England. Public relations executive turned pastor, Jo's previous career included working for Prince Charles as an executive VP of his largest charity. After reaching the pinnacle of the public relations world, Jo felt the call of God to full-time ministry. She is a regular guest on TV and radio shows in the US and UK.

An international speaker and author, Jo ministers with a heart-piercing anointing, sharing with great personal honesty in conferences and at churches around the world. Her passion is to see people set free from all inner hindrances so that they can fulfill their God-given destiny. Countless people have testified to having received powerful and life-changing healing through her ministry. Jo and Paul have two wonderful children, Ben and Abby.

You can connect with Jo via :
jonaughton.com
Facebook (public page - Jo Naughton)
Twitter (@naughtonjo)
Instagram (@naughtonjo)
For more information about Harvest Church London, visit
harvestchurch.org.uk

Also by the Author:

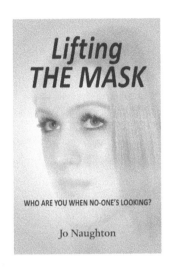

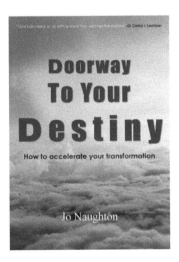

All Jo Naughton's books are available at: <u>jonaughton.com</u>